WHAT REAI

"Until the left rose up to dismantle America, we had the luxury of seeing revival as a good thing—not as a matter of life and death. At this moment, it is unmistakable that all that you and I love about our nation—everything that we hold dear—will be wiped out unless we see a towering, sin-convicting, signs and wonders outbreak. And we are running out of time. *Encounter* is not just a book—it is the right book for this moment. Don't just read it. Absorb into your spirit! It is the word of the Lord for this desperate hour. It sounds the alarm; but more importantly, it infuses us with faith for an awesome intervention of God."

– Mario Murillo
Founder of Living Proof Ministries and best-selling author of
I'm the Christian the Devil Warned You About

"This book is a wake-up call and a must read for anyone who wants to see revival in the church—or in their personal lives. Pastor DiDio's book not only inspires renewed passion but also offers authentic and practical strategies that every Christian can apply to see immediate change. You will not be the same after reading *Encounter*."

– Don Corder
President of The Provisum Group
Author of *Connect: Grow Your Church in 28 Days*

"This work is much needed by the church today. It is a call to repentance from 'lazy Pentecostalism' and secular accommodations into the crucified life of a real Christian. It is a call to holiness and prayer that will result in the revival of the church that the Lord has prepared for us. This work is both prophetic in its corrections and encouraging with its examples. Pastor DiDio shows us the paths we must take through clear writing and examples from both the Bible and heroes of faith, such as Charles Finney, Andrew Murray, and others."

– Dr. William DeArteaga
Christian historian and author of *Quenching the Spirit: Discover the Real Spirit behind the Charismatic Controversy*

"Sometimes the reason we don't get the right answers for the dilemmas we face is because we don't ask the right questions. There are times when we stumble upon the right questions but are not brave enough to accept the answers, especially when they mean we must change a long-standing practice or a firmly held persuasion. Beyond that, there are times when God asks questions of us—and we must always remember, God never asks a question for which He doesn't already know the answer.

"In *Encounter*, Pastor Alan DiDio not only asks penetrating questions, but also provides the necessary solutions—based on biblical truth and time-tested principles—that have brought success to saints throughout the ages. I encourage you to absorb his message so that when God asks you, as He did Gideon, "Have I not sent you?" you will be able to answer with a resounding "Yes!"

– Elder Bill Canfield, World Harvest Church

"Alan has a way of taking the very complex subject of prayer and making it not only understandable, but also desirable and easily applied in your life. This is a must-read for anyone who takes their faith seriously!"

– Doug Garasic
Founder of Rust City Church, author of Notorious

"In every generation God raises up apostolic voices to penetrate the thick darkness that's blanketed society. Pastor Alan DiDio is one of those apostolic voices that's coming to the forefront in this strategic season. *Encounter* is a book I highly recommend and it should be in every believer's personal library. It will prepare you for what's ahead!"

– Brian Taylor
Revival historian

"*Encounter* is for those among us who are done going through the motions of a so-called spiritual life and are ready to reconnect to our power source in our prayer. Pastor Alan has written a book that will help you find the 'more' you're looking for."

–Jeremy Pearson
Pearsons Ministries International

"Pastor Alan DiDio is a modern-day revivalist who ignites a passion for prayer and expectancy in everyone he comes in contact with. His heart for God and his desire for people to experience the miracle-working power of God is unparalleled. Pastor Alan has fulfilled one of the multi-faceted purposes of his life and ministry by writing *Encounter*. Reading this book will take you from where currently are in your spiritual development to where you have always dreamed of being in your walk with God. I highly recommend that you get your pen and highlighter ready and start reading today!"

– Pastor DaVon Alexander
TrueLife Fellowship Church, Matthews, NC

"We desperately need a generation of young people who understand the need for prayer, the power of prayer, and the God who answers prayer. In *Encounter*, Alan DiDio challenges us to pray and dare to believe God for greater things."

– Bishop Ronald A. Ryan,
Pentecostal Church of God, Georgia District

ENCOUNTER

Are You Ready to Experience More
of God's Presence & Power?

ALAN DIDIO

HigherLife Development Services, Inc.

PO Box 623307

Oviedo, Florida 32762

(407) 563-4806

www.ahigherlife.com

Paperback: ISBN # 978-1-7337273-1-0

eBook: ISBN # 978-1-7337273-2-7

CONTENTS

FOREWORD

A serious survey of the twenty-first century church reveals some troubling indicators. Attendance is flat or flagging in many places. Spiritual depth and density among church attendees, and even among some of the clergy, is at what might be an all-time low. Some churches are closing their doors. Some of those that remain are selling out and only emphasizing feeling good instead of the good news of the Bible.

That is why Pastor Alan DiDio, a proud graduate of Valor Christian College, and the message that he proclaims in *Encounter*, is so indispensable in this hour. He is not afraid to confront the problems and pressures of a culture gone mad in forthright fashion. He proves that there is much to be gained by a return to the discarded values of the past, while refusing to be limited to the conventions or expectations of previous generations.

Gideon wondered whether it was possible for a few, or one, to turn the tide of apostasy and anarchy in his generation. He asked the question that not everyone was bold enough or brave enough to ask, then or now: Where is the power? God responded to him directly and dramatically—but the answer was far beyond what Gideon imagined.

Pastor Alan DiDio not only makes the same inquiry that Gideon made, but shows us the solution in unflinching and uncompromising detail. The answer to Gideon's dilemma, and to ours, is as simple in its resolution as it is profound in its implications. *Where is the power?* I challenge you not to ask the question unless you are ready to receive God's riveting and revolutionizing response.

– Dr. Rod Parsley

World Harvest Church, Columbus, Ohio

PREFACE

It was a night I'll never forget. A small group from our church had gathered to seek the face of God. We had entered into worship, and there was a sweet presence in the atmosphere. Some were lifting their hands in praise while others knelt at the altar with tears streaming down their cheeks. I had been left in charge of the prayer meeting that night, and there was much to do. We had an extensive list of items that needed to be covered, but I could feel that God was calling us into a deeper level of prayer.

I could tell that even though people wanted to enter in something was hindering us. It was as though there was some kind of spiritual wall that we could not scale, no matter how hard we tried. As a young minister, I wasn't sure what to do. I tried to exhort and encourage the people to press in, but the truth is that they were already "pressing in." Everyone there that night wanted to go higher and deeper, but none of us knew how to get there. There was a missing ingredient, and we didn't know what it was.

Just when I thought we were going to have to remain in the shallows of our current spiritual experience and go on with the service (and our lives), one of the elders of the church approached me on the stage. The principle that was explained and demonstrated that night has stayed with me for nearly two decades. It was this: Sometimes people can't go deeper in prayer without first receiving an impartation.

What we were missing was an impartation of the spirit of prayer. These leaders had what we needed; and once we received it from them, our lives were radically transformed forever. When I asked what an impartation was,

I was told, "It is when something that is in me gets in you!"

I believe that many Christians are stuck in a malaise, facing spiritual obstacles they see no way around. They want to pray; they want to become everything that God has called them to be, but there's something holding them back. Believers need an impartation to help them rediscover the power of prayer and catapult them into a personal revival.

The search for revival is an uncertain one. Unseen in modern times, this elusive creature of Christian lore often slips into the shadows, and through our fingers, as it easily evades a hapless and inattentive church. Having gone unpreached and therefore undefined, the revival that God has for every believer is often ignored by Christians who have no understanding of its urgency or its power to change everything, and become the fulfillment of every prayer that we have prayed.

We don't need another program to grow the church. We need a revival. We don't need another marriage seminar to mend the broken home. We need a revival. Healing is in revival. Deliverance is in revival. Strength and power are in revival. Revival contains all of these blessings, yet revival can only be initiated and maintained in prayer. Prayer is the fountainhead of all things divine. It is not only urgent, it is also imperative.

How could you find a missing person without a description? How could you search for an item without ever having seen it? As I have grown and developed in ministry, I have learned and relearned this important principle: I need an impartation in order to accomplish everything God wants me to do. That impartation can come in a number of ways; but most importantly, it comes by association with those who have already done whatever it is you hope to accomplish. Follow them as they follow Christ. That is why I recount the revivals of the past in this book. We can look at the hallmarks of those revivals and learn the principles of revival that will serve us today.

If you are reading this book, I believe there's a cry deep down in your spirit—just like there was in Gideon's heart—for more. You want to press in, rediscover your passion, and recover your prayer life. My prayer is that the truth in these pages will impart a fresh revelation of the power of God that is available for you, your family, and the lives of all those around you.

INTRODUCTION

The story of Gideon is the story of the modern church. Today, a new generation stands as a mirror image of this hero of the faith. I believe that everyone reading this book can relate to the same struggles that Gideon faced. Few of us have seen a real move of God, and we have begun to question whether it's even possible.

Were you once deeply passionate about your faith? Have you since become cold, indifferent, possibly even calloused? Has the passion in your heart been quenched by the current mediocrity of the modern church? Have you settled for the norm—just going to church, reading your Bible, trying to live a good life—and, like Gideon, buried God's purpose for your life deep within your subconscious?

Deep down, you know there's more. But every time you try to take one step forward, it seems as though you're pushed two steps backward. You're unsettled, and you feel like there is no way to escape living a life of compromise.

If this describes you, I have good news!

God is about to unleash the winds of change into your life. There's about to be a *revival* in your house. When I say revival, I'm not talking about some week-long church meeting. I'm talking about a divine invasion of your home in which the very climate of your life is transformed to accommodate the blessings of God. God is marshaling His forces. The clarion call is going out. The trumpet is being sounded, and God wants *you*. Will you answer the call? Will you enlist in His army?

If you have been estranged from Him, it's time to rekindle that flickering flame that still burns in your heart. It's time to come out of the muck and mire of mediocrity and take your rightful place on the Rock of Ages.

Do not be mistaken. This book will challenge you. The power of mediocrity is far subtler and more sinister than any other bondage known to man. The only way to be set free is to have a divine encounter. This book was written to set up that meeting!

In Judges 6, when the angel of the Lord appeared to him, Gideon asked him a question, one that resounds in all our hearts: "If I am going to do all You say I am going to do, *where is the power?*" It is a question that expresses a willingness to believe but acknowledges a need for something more. It's a question that will acquaint us with our purpose and inspire the Spirit of God to move on our behalf. If we will earnestly seek God, we will receive an answer to the cry that burned in Gideon's heart: "Where is the power?" My friend, God's answer today is the same as it was to Gideon: "The power is in you!"

WHERE'S THE POWER?

"Every body continues in its state of rest, or of uniform motion in a right line, unless it is compelled to change that state by forces impressed upon it." – Sir Isaac Newton[1]

"How tremendous is the power available to us who believe in God" (Ephesians 1:19, PHILLIPS).

His eyes were fixed as he stared at the fire. It leapt from one field to the next as it consumed not only his family's future, but also his nation's pride. He wanted to run to his mother and feel the comfort that only her arms could bring, but as he looked up into her eyes he didn't see that familiar look of reassurance.

---

1 Isaac Newton, *Mathematical Principles of Natural Philosophy*, vol. 34, 54 vols., The Great Books (Chicago: Encyclopaedia Britannica, 1988), 14.

In desperation, he turned to his father for strength. *My dad is a man of faith*, he said to himself. *Surely, he will be strong, and he will remind us of the promises of our God!* All his life he had heard his father preach about the mighty works of Yahweh. He had heard the story of Abraham, and how God had provided a sacrifice. He could quote the story of Moses and the Red Sea. Many times, when they were in distress, his father would recite these age-old stories. This certainly wasn't the first time they had seen trouble, but there had never been anything like this.

However, as he looked at his father, he saw only a hollow shell of the man he once knew. His hope turned to hopelessness. A mixture of rage, sorrow, and confusion flooded his young mind. *How could this happen? Why doesn't somebody do something?*

His mind began to spin as he heard the cries of his family and felt the pain of his nation simultaneously as they were both overrun by the armies of the Midianites. The smoke from the fire billowed into the sky, blocking the radiance of the sun, along with the promises and traditions they held so dear.

As his eyes locked on the lapping flames, he suddenly felt as though time itself had lost its hold on him. His harsh surroundings all but disappeared; and in that one moment, this young man felt an unusual sense of purpose. He had collided headlong with his destiny.

As quickly as the feeling came, it left. He didn't know how or why, but he knew that greatness awaited him. The innocence of childhood left his face as his brow furrowed and his eyes squinted. He grabbed his father by the shoulders and shook him out of his stupor. "We must leave!" he said. "They'll be back." So, they gathered what was left of their belongings and went into town.

To keep the Israelites from prospering and growing too strong, the Midianites began raiding their homes and burning their fields. Day in and day out, Gideon watched as brave men left the village to gather crops from a field they had hidden from the Midianites. Many never returned. If the enemy found them while they were harvesting crops, they killed them and burned the harvest.

These were dangerous times, and yet Gideon's young mind raced with hope that God would somehow use him to deliver His people from the hand of the Midianites.

"Why God? Why?" was the question many in the village asked as they sat in sackcloth and ashes, crying out for answers. Although he was young, Gideon understood exactly why this had happened. The history and heritage of his people had been effectively passed down. He knew how, in times past, his people had sinned, fallen into bondage, repented, and been delivered. Despite the cyclical lessons of the past, Israel had once again forsaken the God of its fathers, and apostasy was rampant in the land. Gideon knew that sin was the cause, and repentance was its only cure. He watched as God's chosen people worshiped false gods. Even his own family had fallen prey to idolatry and the illusion of peace and safety that it promised.

In a flurry of zeal and compassion, he urged his family to turn from this idolatry and stand up to the onslaught of the enemy. "God is faithful! If we turn to Him, He will defeat our enemy!" But it was to no avail. He was constantly reminded that he was the least in his family and that they were a very weak and poor tribe.

Over time, Gideon himself became estranged from the promises of God. He had heard of the great things his God had done, but he had never actually seen any miracles himself. *Could they have all just been stories?*, he wondered. He had prayed and fasted, but he had never had a divine encounter. Maybe his family was right. Maybe it would be better to just go with the flow.

GIDEON KNEW THAT SIN WAS THE CAUSE, AND REPENTANCE WAS ITS ONLY CURE.

After some time, Gideon gave up all hope of leading his people into victory. There was overwhelming pressure from his family and friends to be *normal*. Because of this pressure, Gideon buried his call to greatness deep within his subconscious.

Attempting to fill the void caused by the neglect of his calling, he settled for the most feared job in the village. He did what few were willing to do: He became a harvester. Daily he would sneak away to the old winepresses. These places always reminded him of better days. The winepresses were symbols of a time when his nation was prosperous and at peace. Now they were used as hideaways to sift whatever wheat they managed to harvest. Gideon often spent his days in the winepress in earnest prayer as he worked. *Why would God allow this to happen? Where are all the miracles I've heard about?* He didn't know that he was about to have a divine encounter.

That encounter is described in Judges 6:

> *And there came an angel of the Lord, and sat under an oak which was in Ophrah, that pertained unto Joash the Abiezrite:*

and his son Gideon threshed wheat by the winepress, to hide it from the Midianites. And the angel of the LORD appeared unto him, and said unto him, The LORD is with thee, thou mighty man of valour (Judges 6:11–12).

At this point, Gideon was surely wondering if the angel of the Lord knew who he really was. A mighty man of valor? Hardly! Here he was, hiding from the Midianites. However, as long as the angel of the Lord was talking to him, he decided to press the issue a little further and see if he could get some answers to their dilemma.

And Gideon said unto him, Oh my LORD, if the LORD be with us, why then is all this befallen us? and where be all his miracles which our fathers told us of, saying, Did not the LORD bring us up from Egypt? but now the LORD hath forsaken us, and delivered us into the hands of the Midianites. And the LORD looked upon him, and said, Go in this thy might, and thou shalt save Israel from the hand of the Midianites: have not I sent thee? (Judges 6:13—14).

This was not the answer he was expecting! He was hoping to hear that God was going to send someone to intervene and save his family and his people. He was shocked to hear that *he* was going to be that someone!

And he said unto him, Oh my LORD, wherewith shall I save Israel? behold, my family is poor in Manasseh, and I am the least in my father's house. And the LORD said unto him, Surely I will be with thee, and thou shalt smite the Midianites as one man (Judges 6:15–16).

In a flash of recollection, Gideon's mind went back to the time he had first felt the stirrings of his destiny. Could it really be true—that God was with him? There was just one question left to answer.

His response to the angel of the Lord was to ask the same question we are asking today. The cry of his heart is the cry of all our hearts. It's a question that will acquaint us with our purpose and inspire the Spirit of God to move on our behalf. If we will earnestly seek God, we too will receive an answer to the cry that burned in Gideon's heart: *Where is the power?*

TIME TO REDISCOVER THE POWER

It began as a normal Vacation Bible School organized by the Loman Mennonite Church in Minnesota. The year was 1954. Seventy-six teenagers from seven churches gathered together between Christmas and New Year's to pray and study the Bible. The leader of the event was a man named Gerald Derstine, a local Mennonite pastor.

Pastor Derstine could tell that this was going to be a successful event when, on the first night, thirteen youth were gloriously saved. Thirteen salvations by today's overachieving standards may not sound like much. Far more important, though, than the quantity of those saved, was the quality of their encounter with Christ. These young people had a true divine encounter.

As these young people committed their lives to Christ, the Spirit of God began to move in ways to which these Mennonites were unaccustomed. Some children "reported hearing angels singing." Others were gripped by heavy intercession for their unsaved parents. The pastors overseeing the event were certainly impressed with this sudden flood of devotion, but they were unprepared for what would happen next. Students began to fall prostrate on the floor, trembling under the power of God and speaking in unknown tongues. Fearful of demonic influences, the leaders started to plead the blood and pray; but the more they pled the blood, the stronger it became! This is what the pastor wrote:

"The little clock in the back of the church was ticking away, into the wee hours of the morning, when our first assurance came that this was indeed a work of God. Skip, the first boy who had come crying to the front, stopped the strange jabbering and began to speak intelligibly. A radiant smile lit up his face as he began to clearly articulate one word at a time. He spoke so slowly and so softly we had to lean close to hear what he was saying. His body was relaxed and peaceful now but his eyes remained closed as he said in a gentle, barely audible voice, 'Turn–in–your–Bibles–to Acts 2:17–and–18–and–you–shall–under–stand.'

"I quickly reached for my Bible. Thank God, at least he was saying something scriptural. My fingers trembled as I leafed through to the book of Acts, chapter 2, verses 17 and 18. I began reading to the small cluster of people who had gathered around the boy:

"'And it shall come to pass in the last days, saith God, I will pour out of my Spirit upon all flesh: and your sons and your daughters shall prophesy, and your young men shall see visions, and your old men shall dream dreams: And on my servants and on my handmaidens, I will pour out in those days of my Spirit; and they shall prophesy.'

"I stared at the words in astonishment. Then I looked at the boy and back at the verses again. Could all this truly be the work of God? In fact, could it be possible that this was the very revival we had been praying and fasting for? I wanted to believe it. Yet it was contrary to our doctrine. We had always been taught that these particular Scriptures had been fulfilled in Bible days. I read over the passage once more. 'In the last days—'

"'Brother Derstine! Come over here. Connie's saying something.' I hurried over to the side of the young girl who was still lying on the floor. She also had a heavenly smile on her face and was talking. She spoke authoritatively, one word at a time, as she told of an 'end-time revival' such as the world had never seen. Her friends, hovering over her, leaned close to catch every word. On their faces was a mixture of bewilderment and relief.

"By that time the other young people who had been lying on the floor, 'speaking in tongues' and trembling, became still and one by one they began to speak. Some of them sang. Others described heavenly scenes complete with elaborate descriptive gestures. Yet they all still lay on the floor, eyes closed, in a trance. There were prophecies of impending world events. (These particularly bothered me. We were only interested in revival for our own community.) There were words of exhortation and passages of Scripture. As each one ended his message almost invariably he would say, 'This is my body you see, this is my voice you hear, but this is from the Lord.'"[2]

Under the influence of the Holy Spirit, these teenagers recited Scriptures they didn't know, prophesied future world events, and encountered the living Christ. One teen even prophesied that Billy Graham would one day

---

2 Gerald Derstine and Joanne Derstine, *Following the Fire* (Orlando, FL: Orlando: Bridge-Logos Publishers, 1980), used by permission.

preach behind the Iron Curtain. This was in 1954![3]

In *Following the Fire*, Derstine recounts the prayer and fasting that led to this mighty move of God, the persecution that followed, and the revival that ensued. Oh, how we need an infusion of this kind of power in the church today!

Some years ago, I had the privilege of meeting Gerald Derstine. Since that revival, he has gone on to establish more than six thousand churches on every continent of the world. I asked him, "What is the most important message that the church needs to hear today?"

This general of the faith said to me, with passion in his eyes, "The church today needs a revelation of the Christ, the Anointed One." That moment has stayed with me throughout the years. The church needs to rediscover the power available in the presence and person of Jesus the Christ.

---

3 Vinson Synan, *Century of the Holy Spirit: 100 Years of Pentecostal and Charismatic Renewal, 1901-2001* (Nashville, TN: Thomas Nelson, 2001).

CHAPTER 1: QUESTIONS FOR REFLECTION

1. In our opening story, a young Gideon has a flash of insight into his future. Have you ever felt that there was a higher purpose for your life? Describe this.

2. Gideon was hiding in a winepress to thresh wheat because he feared the Midianites. Has fear influenced your response to the will of God in some way in the past? How? Be specific.

3. Why was Gideon so surprised when the angel of the Lord called him, "a mighty man of valor"? How would you respond if God said this to you?

4. Gerald Derstine said, "The church today needs a revelation of the Christ, the Anointed One." How would that revelation create an atmosphere for revival in our churches and our lives?

Chapter 2

THE MISSING INGREDIENT

"Persons need not and ought not to set any bounds to their spiritual and gracious appetites, [instead they ought] to be endeavoring by all possible ways to inflame their desires and to obtain more spiritual pleasures…

Our hungerings and thirstings after God and Jesus Christ and after holiness can't be too great for the value of these things, for they are things of infinite value… [Therefore] endeavor to promote spiritual appetites by laying yourself in the way of allurement… There is no such thing as excess in our taking of this spiritual food. There is no such virtue as temperance in spiritual feasting."

—Jonathan Edwards[1]

"We thought that we had the answers, it was the questions we had wrong." —Bono[2]

---

1 Adrian Warnock, "QUOTE - Jonathan Edwards on Hungering After More of God," *Patheos*, October 28, 2006, accessed January 25, 2019, https://www.patheos.com/blogs/adrianwarnock/2006/10/quote-jonathan-edwards-on-hungering-after-more-of-god/, quoted in John Piper, *What Jesus Demands from the World* (Wheaton, ILL: Crossway, 2006), 90.

2 Bono, "Bono Quotes," *BrainyQuote*, accessed January 25, 2019, https://www.brainyquote.com/quotes/bono_129881.

The Tournament of Roses parade has a long-standing tradition. On New Year's morning we get to see those elaborate floats—which have taken nearly a year to construct—paraded through the city streets. It's quite a show, and it draws the attention of millions around the world.

One year, a stunning float came to a sputtering stop in the middle of the street. It was out of gas! Can you imagine the embarrassment? The entire parade was held up until someone could help them get refueled.

The awkwardness of the moment quickly turned to humiliation as the crowd discovered that the offending float represented the Standard Oil Company. The company whose business was power had run out of power![3]

As a teenager, I had convinced myself that I was an atheist. As ridiculous a conclusion as that is, I didn't come to it on my own. I had the help of lots and lots of Christians. I like to call them "Christian atheists." To me, a "Christian atheist" is someone who claims to believe in God but who lives like He doesn't exist. Do you know anyone like that? These people may attend church and even read their Bibles, yet they are complete strangers to the God they claim to worship.

On the surface they look good, but underneath all the stereotypes they've worked so feverishly to maintain, they're empty. With no spiritual depth or scriptural foundation, these Christian atheists are holding up the parade. What's worse is that an entire generation is watching them. As a teenager reared in the buckle of the Bible Belt, I saw their hypocrisy for myself as they sat in judgment over others completely blind to the beam in their own eye. I wondered, *If their God is real, why are they so depressed and bitter?*

---

3 Adapted from Max Lucado, *God Came Near: God's Perfect Gift* (Portland, OR: Multnomah Press, 1987), 95.

I knew instinctively that if Christianity isn't *supernatural*, then it must be *superficial*.

Don't get me wrong, I wanted it all to be true. I wanted to believe the Bible, but the God of the Bible and the God of the modern Christian were often at odds with one another. Gideon wanted it all to be true, but he had never seen a miracle. He had heard plenty of stories, but Gideon had no living example to show him a God who is the "same yesterday, and to day, and for ever" (Hebrews 13:8). Judges 2:10 describes this generation perfectly:

> *And there arose another generation after them, which knew not the LORD, nor yet the works which He had done (Judges 2:10).*

Like Gideon, we are living in a Judges 2:10 generation. It's true, isn't it? When speaking of the current condition of the church, it is impossible to avoid words like: *lifeless, impotent, self-absorbed, ineffective, useless, unproductive,* and *vain*. This is not an attempt to point the finger, nor should we look down our long religious noses at those we consider to be "lesser-lights." (The lesser light rules the night: the pale moonlight is but a reflection of the sun's glorious light).

This is a call for radical introspection. For too long, we've heard fiery messages full of conviction, and thought of all the people we know who needed to hear them. This Word isn't for them! Gideon's cry is for you, and it is for me.

Our problem is not that our fortifications have been torn down or that we are surrounded and outnumbered by the Enemy—because neither one is true. Our demise is not due to battle-worn and weary saints who are hardpressed on the right and yielding at the center of the battle line. Our failure is found in the fact that no one seems to be able to find the battlefield any-more or even acknowledge that there is a battle that needs to be fought!

It seems like we've managed to deceive ourselves into believing that we have somehow created a truce with our enemies. Every day we hope and pray that they keep their end of the bargain. If that isn't bad enough, we're also troubled by anyone who may suggest that the battle is still on or that God is still looking for soldiers willing to give their lives for the cause of Christ.

The truth of the matter is that the Enemy is not at the gate. He is already *within our borders* —populating our schools, sitting in seats of power, at-tending our churches, and even sleeping in our own beds. Many would rath-er hang on to their tedious traditions than turn over the tables the way our Savior did.

In times like these church attendance skyrockets while spirituality de-clines to record-breaking lows. As the House of Bread (the church) ex-periences its own famine, we stay open for business saying, "Let all who will, come!" The problem is that when the world shows up—starving at our doorstep—they discover it was just a mirage and a scam. Their cry be-comes, "Where is the bread?"

This is the underlying reason for much of the animosity directed at Chris-tianity today. The world wanted us to be as anointed and free as we claimed; but when they showed up, they discovered that we were just as bad off as they were. Nothing makes people angrier than when they have their hopes dashed into pieces. They wanted it to be true. They still want it to be true.

Luckily, many of us—like Gideon—are still searching for the answer.

Many of us refuse to buy into the lie that this is the way it has to be. We realize that what Jesus taught on this earth and what He bought on that cross spoke of more than a social event added to our weekly calendars. The God we serve is no respecter of persons. If He did it before, He'll do it once more!

For the sake of the hurting and for the cause of Christ, let's make the decision today that we will no longer shrink back into the shadows and allow the Enemy to use our own stagnation as a poison. We spend so much of our time attempting to look like Christians that we rarely take the time to actually become Christlike. It's time for us to become the change we desire to see.

MIGHT? WHAT MIGHT?

The angel's response to Gideon's cry is astounding: "Go in this thy might!" What was the angel talking about? What might? Gideon had no power, no money, no influence, and no physical strength. All Gideon had was a question: Where is the power?

It appears as though the question itself holds some secret to the origin of Gideon's so-called might. This should come as no surprise when we consider that Jesus Himself declared:

> *Blessed are they which do hunger and thirst after righteousness: for they shall be filled (Matthew 5:6).*

In this verse, Jesus taught that hunger can accomplish what a lifetime of study never will. Hunger connects us to spiritual things. Hunger prophesies fulfillment.

Over the years, I have had the opportunity to share the gospel in many nations around the world. When I think of hunger, I think of Guatemala. Though I have been in more destitute places like Haiti and Pakistan, my time in Guatemala marked me forever.

I had the opportunity to visit a local garbage dump. It was not unlike the vile-smelling, disease-infested dumps we have in the United States—with one exception: there were hundreds of people—many of them children— digging through the trash looking for food. As the garbage trucks rolled into this dump, everyone swarmed around them. While the trucks were still moving, I saw mothers toss their young children up into the back of the truck, with the hope that they would be the first to get hold of a half-eaten piece of bread or an unfinished bottle of water. It is amazing what true hunger will drive people to do.

As jarring as that scene was, it was far worse to see the children who sat idle. As everyone else fought to satisfy their hunger, these children were so malnourished that they could no longer sense the hunger within them; and therefore didn't feel the need or have the energy to pursue fulfillment. Does that sound familiar?

> *Behold, the days come, saith the LORD GOD, that I will send a famine in the land, not a famine of bread, nor a thirst for water, but of hearing the words of the LORD (Amos 8:11).*

The Book of Amos sets forth an intriguing prophecy that one can easily overlook and understate. The prophet Amos declares that there will be a famine that defies logic. In this famine, there'll be plenty of bread and water. Amos declares that the scarcity will be found in the hearing of the Word of God. I believe that we are seeing this prophecy fulfilled every day in our own lives.

It is particularly important to note that God did not say that there would be a famine of the *Word* of God. In our modern technological society, no one in America is without access to the living, life-giving Word of God if they really want it. With a plethora of Christian books, CDs, downloads, apps, TV shows, radio programs, and podcasts, there is a hearty helping of God's Word available to all. That's not what the Holy Spirit's warning said. Amos warned that there would come a day when there would be a shortage of *hearing* the Word of the Lord.

OUR DILEMMA TODAY IS FINDING PEOPLE WHO ARE HUNGRY ENOUGH TO DILIGENTLY SEEK HIM AND DISCOVER FOR THEMSELVES WHAT HE IS SAYING.

God is our Provider, and He has promised to give us an ample supply of whatever we need even before we need it. The problem has not been getting God to speak. Our dilemma today is finding people who are hungry enough to diligently seek Him and discover for themselves what He is saying.

> *But without faith it is impossible to please him: for he that cometh to God must believe that he is, and that he is a rewarder of them that diligently seek him (Hebrews 11:6).*

One dictionary defines hunger as, "a feeling of discomfort or weakness caused by the lack of food, coupled with the desire to eat."[4] In order for there to be hunger, there must be both discomfort and desire.

Are we comfortable with our current spiritual life?

Hunger begins with discomfort. Too many Christians are comfortable in their own stagnation. Like Gideon, we've grown numb to our discomfort and have been satisfied with threshing a day's worth of wheat when God has called us to rescue a generation. If we are Christians, we have been called by God to do the impossible. We have been commissioned to explore the supernatural. The mediocre, the mundane, and the norm will bore us, cause us to be unsettled, and eventually produce a frustration and agitation that only a divine encounter can fix.

If we want to tap into "this thy might," we must learn to recognize spiritual discomfort. If we are constantly on edge, aggravated, or anxious it may be our unfulfilled spirit crying out to be fed.

As a pastor, I see this with men all the time—especially when I'm counseling couples. If a man is not accomplishing something significant in his life, he'll often become agitated, troubled, and angry for seemingly no reason and it spills over into his marriage. Instead of suppressing this discomfort, I encourage them to recognize it for what it is: the neglect of purpose. Once discomfort has been recognized for what it truly is, we can begin to articulate our desire.

What things soever ye desire, when ye pray, believe that ye receive them, and ye shall have them (Mark 11:24).

---

4 "Hunger | Definition of Hunger in English by *Oxford Dictionaries*," Oxford Dictionaries | English, accessed August 24, 2018, https://en.oxforddictionaries.com/definition/hunger.

Absent or improper desires are the reasons many Christians don't get their prayers answered. Answers are servants to questions. Before you can get the answer that you desire, you must first define the real need. Many Christians have no idea what they really need.

I once heard someone talking about taking their child to a toy store. The child had been given some birthday money and wanted to spend it before it burned a hole in his pocket. The nine-year-old rushed through the store as though he were on a scavenger hunt. When he found what he wanted, he proclaimed, "I *need* that!" Regrettably, he had only been given fifty dollars, and the toy was priced at eighty dollars. When his dad tried to gently prod him in another direction due to the lack of funds, the young man said, "But I *need* that!"

For parents, this situation is all too familiar. I like the way this dad responded. He said, "Son, you don't *need* that toy. That toy is eighty dollars. All you have is fifty dollars. What you really *need* is thirty dollars."

One hurdle to possessing the kind of hunger that prophesies fulfillment is not knowing what we really need. I've spoken with many people who thought they *needed* to be "blessed," but what they really needed was an encounter with God. Many may think they need financial provision, but what they really need is wisdom from the Word of God.

> *Ye ask, and receive not, because ye ask amiss, that ye may consume it upon your lusts (James 4:3).*

If we can learn to recognize our real need, we can appropriately focus our desires, so that Mark 11:24 and Matthew 5:4 can be fulfilled in our lives.

What is it that we really *need*? We need to accomplish God's will and discover His intention. We need a revival. Regardless of how impossible it may seem or how unworthy we may feel, we will never have peace until we are pursuing His purpose.

WHEN DISCOMFORT WITH OUR CURRENT CONDITION COLLIDES WITH A DESIRE FOR GOD'S RADICAL WILL, HUNGER IS BORN

When discomfort with our current condition collides with a desire for God's radical will, hunger is born—and Jesus promised to fill the hungry.

Gideon's cry was an impassioned plea from a hungry heart. God's answer was the same then as it is today: "Go in this thy might!" The *might* that Gideon discovered was that hunger for change brought answers and fulfillment. It is hunger that keeps the heart seeking. Luke 11:9 promises that everyone who seeks, find*s*. Let's keep seeking. Let's allow our hunger to drive us into an experience with God that we never dreamed imaginable. God is raising up an army of hungry hearts who are unashamed and are willing to cry, "Where is the power?"

CHAPTER 2: QUESTIONS FOR REFLECTION

1. According to the author, what is a "Christian atheist"? Could you ever be mistaken for one? Why or why not?

2. What does the author mean when he talks about a famine in the "house of bread"? What does this look like in a local church?

3. We know what natural hunger feels like. What are the characteristics of spiritual hunger?

4. Luke 11:9 promises that everyone who seeks, finds. What have you been seeking from the Lord? How, and why? Have you found it yet?

Chapter 3
MUCH NEEDED R & R, PART 1

"Still later he appeared to the eleven disciples as they were eating to-gether. He rebuked them for their stubborn unbelief" (Mark 16:14, NLT).

"If we put off repentance another day, we have a day more to repent of, and a day less to repent in." —William Mason[1]

A war-weary nation was facing another impending conflict, social unrest was at its peak, and there was a major stock market crash. The inevitable un-certainty facing millions of people led them to seek solace in alcohol, gam-bling, and other vices. Coarse sensuality seemed to pervade every aspect of society, and many women refused to go out after sunset for fear of being

1 Charles Haddon Spurgeon, "Psalm 95:7 Commentary - The Treasury of David," *Bible Study Tools*, accessed January 25, 2019, https://www.biblestudytools.com/commentaries/treasury-of-david/psalms-95-7.html.

assaulted. Though this may sound a lot like our current cultural climate, this was the condition of our beloved nation in the early 1800s.

Every generation has its own yoke of bondage, but every generation also has its own anointing to destroy that yoke. On October 10, 1821, God placed His hand on a young lawyer named Charles Grandison Finney as he prayed alone in the woods in Adams, New York. This man would become a mighty weapon in the hand of God. Like Gideon, he confronted the powerlessness of the church in his search for a genuine move of God. Even before his conversion, he questioned the superficiality of the modern (in those days) Christian church.

Once, a local church member asked Finney if he would like the church to pray for him. His response was very Gideonesque:

"No! Because I do not see that God answers your prayers. I suppose that I need to be prayed for, for I am conscious that I am a sinner; but I do not see that it will do any good for you to pray for me; for you are continually asking, but you do not receive. You have been praying for revival of religion ever since I came to Adams, and yet you have it not. You have been praying for the Holy Ghost to descend upon yourselves, and yet complaining of your leanness. You have prayed enough since I have attended these meetings to have prayed the devil out of Adams, if there is any virtue in your prayers. But here you are praying on and complaining still."[2]

Finney's statement does hit a little too close to home, even today, doesn't it? On the evening of the day of his conversion, Finney was in his office when he had a vision and fell weeping at the feet of Jesus.

---

2 Charles G. Finney, Richard A. G. Dupuis, and Garth Rosell, *The Original Memoirs of Charles G. Finney* (Grand Rapids, MI: Zondervan, 2002), 10.

"I received a mighty baptism of the Holy Ghost... Without expecting it, without ever having the thought in my mind that there was such a thing for me, without any recollection that I had ever heard the thing mentioned by any person in the world, at a moment entirely unexpected by me, the Holy Spirit descended upon me in a manner that seemed to go through me body and soul."[3]

This encounter set Charles G. Finney on fire, and from this time on thousands would gather just to watch him burn. Buildings would be filled to the rafters, and without introduction or song he would walk to the pulpit and quote a verse like this one found in Isaiah 3:

> *Say ye to the righteous, that it shall be well with him: for they shall eat the fruit of their doings. Woe unto the wicked! It shall be ill with him: for the reward of his hands shall be given him (Isaiah 3:10–11).*

His hearers became so convicted that even after the meeting, people tried to find where he was staying so that they could get him to pray for them. Meetings continued in schoolhouses, church buildings, and even barrooms that had been closed because the owner had been born again. Even though it was harvest time, farmers came in from their fields for Finney's 1 P.M. service. A large percentage of people in every city he preached in were converted.

Finney went to a village called Sodom in New York that was so named because of how rowdy those who settled it were. There had never been a religious service in Sodom before Finney came. After fifteen minutes of his

---

3 Ibid. 22–24.

preaching, the congregation began to fall from their seats; they fell in every direction and cried for mercy. Finney stated, "If I had a sword in each hand, I could not have cut them off their seats as fast as they fell. The whole crowd was either on their knees or prostrate. Everyone prayed for himself, if they were able to speak at all. I, of course, was obliged to stop preaching, for they no longer paid any attention."[4]

We need another Great Awakening in America today, but God will only send it to hungry Gideon-like hearts.

THE LOST AXE HEAD

Roughly three hundred years after Gideon's encounter with God, another man came bursting onto the scene with the same kind of hunger in his heart. His name was Elisha, and he was the kind of living example Gideon would have welcomed. At that time, there were many young men whose souls were crying out for an encounter with the divine, and when they met this living legend named Elisha, they wanted to follow him wherever he went. These youngsters were called the "sons of the prophets" and they were an enthusiastic bunch. In 2 Kings 6, their zeal was in full force as they pled with Elisha to allow them to build a place big enough for all of them to live. They wanted to stay as close to the power of God as possible. It wasn't a bad idea, so Elisha consented. They worked tirelessly to cut down the trees needed for the construction of their new home.

Everything was going swimmingly until one young man lost his power.

---

4 Charles Grandison Finney, "Memoirs of Revivals of Religion," *The Gospel Truth,* accessed January 25, 2019, http://gospeltruth.net/1868Memoirs/memoirsindex.htm.

While he was felling a tree by the river, his axe head came off and fell into the water. What good is an axe handle without an axe head? To top it all off, the axe was borrowed, and the owner wasn't going to be happy when he found out that it was broken. This young man quickly ran to Elisha, who understood what had happened and had a solution. Here's a description:

> But as one was felling a beam, the axe head fell into the water: and he cried, and said, Alas, master! for it was borrowed. And the man of God said, Where fell it? And he shewed him the place. And he cut down a stick, and cast it in thither; and the iron did swim. Therefore said he, Take it up to thee. And he put out his hand, and took it (2 Kings 6:5–7).

Once again, we see that the question drives us to the answer. The man of God essentially asks the young man the same question Gideon asked, "Where fell it?" or "Where did you lose your power?" The power we require will not come through some newfangled method. It's important to realize that the power we need has already been given to us—it just got lost somewhere along the way. Understanding this critical reality will keep us from error and will focus our search in the right direction. One of the most self-defeating things a Christian can do is to pray for what he or she already has.

THE POWER WE NEED HAS ALREADY BEEN GIVEN TO US—IT JUST GOT LOST SOMEWHERE ALONG THE WAY

Once there was a man who purchased a chainsaw from the local hardware store. After a week, he brought it back to the store, completely flustered. The man slammed the chainsaw on the counter and said, "This thing is a piece of junk!" The store clerk replied, "What's seems to be the problem?" The man complained, "I've been working all week with this thing, and I haven't been able to cut down one tree. I want my money back!" The clerk examined the chainsaw, checked its blade, and cranked it up. The roar of the perfectly operational chainsaw filled the store. When the clerk turned it off, the confused man asked, "What was that noise?"

We have been working with a giant chainsaw that we haven't even turned on—and we've been complaining about the results. Our axe head has fallen off, but we just keep on swinging at the trees. In frustration, we turn to new methods and innovative strategies, not knowing that we've had what we needed all along.

Yes, Isaiah 43:19 declares that God desires to do a "new thing," but it is not referring to something new to God or new to mankind; it's just new to us. Ecclesiastes 1:9 says that, "the thing that hath been, it is that which shall be...there is no new thing under the sun."

Listen to Paul's prayer for the church at Ephesus:

> *Wherefore I also, after I heard of your faith in the LORD Jesus, and love unto all the saints, cease not to give thanks for you, making mention of you in my prayers; that the God of our LORD Jesus Christ, the Father of glory, may give unto you the spirit of wisdom and revelation in the knowledge of him: the eyes of your understanding being enlightened; that ye may know what is the hope of his calling, and what the riches of the glory of his*

inheritance in the saints, and what is the exceeding greatness of his power to us-ward who believe, according to the working of his mighty power, which he wrought in Christ, when he raised him from the dead, and set him at his own right hand in the heavenly places, far above all principality, and power, and might, and dominion, and every name that is named, not only in this world, but also in that which is to come: and hath put all things under his feet, and gave him to be the head over all things to the church, which is his body, the fulness of him that filleth all in all (Ephesians 1:15–23).

This is truly eye-opening. Paul doesn't pray for God to give the Ephesian church anything new. Paul doesn't pray for God to do *anything* for the church at Ephesus either. What does he pray for? "The spirit of wisdom and revelation in the knowledge of him: The eyes of their understanding being enlightened; that they may know." He prayed for wisdom, revelation, knowledge, eyes of understanding, and enlightenment that we may *know*! Paul doesn't pray for God to do or give anything new because everything we need has already been provided in Christ:

Blessed be the God and Father of our LORD Jesus Christ, who hath blessed us with all spiritual blessings in heavenly places in Christ (Ephesians 1:3).

Paul knew what few ever learn—God has already blessed us with all the power we need, and all we have to do is find it. Everything our spirit cries out for has already been provided, granted, transferred, and transmitted into our possession as an inheritance in Jesus Christ, but it's been neglected by the church, cast off by our own carnality, and hidden by our Enemy. Gideon knew that what had been, could be again—if he could just find it.

HOW DO WE FIND WHAT'S BEEN LOST?

If we will look at what *has been,* then we can know what *will be.* We can learn from the successes and failures of the past. This is why there's some much-needed R & R in the body of Christ today. By R & R, I don't mean *rest & recreation.* We've had plenty of that. What we need is some *repentance,* and even a good *rebuke.* These two conveniently overlooked keys will assist us in going back to where we lost our power.

> **IF REPENTANCE IS THE KEY TO RECLAIMING LOST POWER, THEN A GOOD REBUKE WILL ALWAYS BE THE BEGINNING OF RESTORATION.**

There's only one portal through which mankind can travel into the past and reclaim what's been lost: *repentance.* It's only through the narrow corridors of repentance that we can find our way back and rediscover the foundations. The pathway of repentance is becoming less and less traveled as popular church culture steers farther and farther away from all forms of accountability.

This is truly tragic because one of the only ways to discover real repentance is through the doorway of a rebuke. If repentance is the key to reclaiming lost power, then a good rebuke will always be the beginning of restoration.

In the award-winning movie *Forrest Gump,* our beloved star reminisces about the first time he was introduced to the love of his life: "From that day on, we was always together. Jenny and me was like peas and carrots."[5] Similarly, and sometimes regrettably, rebuke and repentance go together like peas and carrots. The reality is that it's hard to have true repentance without a good rebuke.

> *Then the channels of waters were seen, and the foundations of the world were discovered at thy rebuke, O Lord, at the blast of the breath of thy nostrils (Psalm 18:15).*

In a time when we have had our fill of megalomaniac pastors and maniacal church leaders, the idea of submitting to a rebuke is repulsive to most. However, the Bible still says that the "foundations" can be discovered at God's rebuke. Isn't that what we're after? If what we desire is a foundation that has already been laid, then what we need is a proper rebuke that will trigger godly repentance which will, in turn, get us to where we want to go and need to be.

---

5 Forrest Gump, dir. Robert Zemeckis, perf. Tom Hanks. Hollywood: Paramount Pictures, 1994.

CHAPTER 3: QUESTIONS FOR REFLECTION

1. Charles Finney rebuked church attendees in his hometown because he didn't see any results from their prayers. Would he say the same thing about you? Why or why not?

2. Elisha asked the worker who lost his axe head, "Where fell it?" What does the axe head represent? Why is this question still relevant today?

3. Why did Paul pray the way he did for the church at Ephesus? How would praying this way help you?

4. Have you ever received a rebuke? How did it help you?

5. Do you remember where you lost your axe head? Are you ready to get it back?

Chapter 4

MUCH NEEDED R & R, PART 2

"Now no chastening for the present seemeth to be joyous, but grievous: nevertheless afterward it yieldeth the peaceable fruit of righteousness unto them which are exercised thereby" (Hebrews 12:11).

"The man whose little sermon is 'repent' sets himself against his age, and will for the time being be battered mercilessly by the age whose moral tone he challenges. There is but one end for such a man—'off with his head!' You had better not try to preach repentance until you have pledged your head to heaven." —Joseph Parker[1]

We all believe that the Great Commission is a vital aspect of our Christian lives, don't we? Well, we should! In the Great Commission, we see the heart of the Father clearly expressed and the mission of the church plainly articulated:

---

1 Leonard Ravenhill, *Why Revival Tarries* (Minneapolis, MN: Bethany House, 1986), 98.

And he said unto them, Go ye into all the world, and preach the gospel to every creature. He that believeth and is baptized shall be saved; but he that believeth not shall be damned. And these signs shall follow them that believe; in my name shall they cast out devils; they shall speak with new tongues; they shall take up serpents; and if they drink any deadly thing, it shall not hurt them; they shall lay hands on the sick, and they shall recover. So then after the Lord had spoken unto them, he was received up into heaven, and sat on the right hand of God. And they went forth, and preached every where, the Lord working with them, and confirming the word with signs following. Amen (Mark 16:15–20).

It's obvious that without the Great Commission, the church would be lost. But did you know that the Great Commission was given as a rebuke? Whenever people picture Jesus speaking to His disciples, they often imagine a lovable figure floating on a cloud speaking in mellow tones with coffee in one hand and wrapped in a blanket. The truth is that there were times when He was frustrated with His followers. This was one of those times.

After His resurrection, Jesus first appeared to Mary Magdalene. When she told the disciples about it, they did not believe her. Following that, He appeared to two of His followers as they walked and talked. When these two told the other disciples about this, they didn't believe them either!

It is no wonder then that when Jesus appeared to the eleven remaining disciples—the story is recorded in Mark 16—that He rebuked their unbelief:

Afterward he appeared unto the eleven as they sat at meat,

*and upbraided them with their unbelief and hardness of heart,
because they believed not them which had seen him after he was
risen (Mark 16:14).*

Jesus had already commissioned them, but a lot had happened since that time, and they had lost their sense of purpose. The resurrected Christ then appears before His would-be apostles and helps them rediscover their power. How does He do it? He rebukes them for their unbelief, follows that by reminding them that their purpose was to go into all the world and preach the gospel, *and* that He would be working with them, "confirming the word with signs following." This concept is explained in more detail in Hebrews:

And have you forgotten the encouraging words God spoke to you as his children? He said, "My child, don't make light of the LORD's discipline, and don't give up when he corrects you. For the Lord disciplines those he loves, and he punishes each one he accepts as his child."

As you endure this divine discipline, remember that God is treating you as his own children. Who ever heard of a child who is never disciplined by its father? If God doesn't discipline you as he does all of his children, it means that you are illegitimate and are not really his children at all. Since we respected our earthly fathers who disciplined us, shouldn't we submit even more to the discipline of the Father of our spirits, and live forever?

For our earthly fathers disciplined us for a few years, doing the best they knew how. But God's discipline is always good for us, so that we might share in his holiness. No discipline is enjoyable while it is happening—it's painful! But afterward there will be a peaceful harvest of right living for those who are trained in this way (Hebrews 12:5–11, NLT).

When we begin to understand the freedom that comes through a rebuke and through repentance we'll become gluttons for divine punishment. I'm not recommending that we allow ourselves to be railroaded or demeaned by some carnal "spiritual" leader, but if we want to discover the power of repentance we have to allow the Lord of our lives to be honest with us about every aspect of our lives.

A REAL REBUKE IS SIMPLY A LOVING NUDGE OUT OF DARKNESS TOWARD LIGHT.

Arthur W. Pink, a renowned English Bible teacher said:

"The nature of Christ's salvation is woefully misrepresented by the present-day evangelist. He announces a Savior from Hell rather than a Savior from sin. And that is why so many are fatally deceived, for there are multitudes who wish to escape the lake of fire who have no desire to be delivered from their carnality and worldliness."[2]

A rebuke is not supposed to be a condescending charge brought against someone to make them feel unworthy. A real rebuke is simply a loving nudge out of darkness toward light. When a godly rebuke is responded to in faith, it lifts a weight and brings in a breath of fresh air. A rebuke is an occasion for a new beginning, an opportunity to rediscover the foundations.

---

2 A. W. Pink, "The Nature of Christ's Salvation Misrepresented by the Present-day "Evangelist." - Sermon Index," *SermonIndex Audio Sermons*, accessed January 31, 2019, http://www.sermonindex.net/modules/articles/index.php?view=article&aid=730.

REPENT FOR THE KINGDOM IS AT HAND

As a parent, I'm responsible for disciplining my children in love. I have two amazing kids, but no matter how wonderful they may be, from time to time they need a nudge in the right direction. When we discipline our children, think about how we would like them to react to our correction. Do we want them to whine and beat themselves up with condemnation? Of course not! How many of us have said, "This is going to hurt me more than it hurts you?" That statement sounds ridiculous to a child, but once we become parents, our hearts ache when our child experiences any type of pain or distress. Our love for them is beyond their comprehension. If they only knew what we were trying to save them from, they'd repent and listen the first time—but alas, kids will be kids!

All we want is for our children to receive our correction and grow thereby. We just want to make their lives easier. The same is true for our loving heavenly Father. In Isaiah 54:9, God promises that He will never be angry with us again. In Lamentations 3:33, He says that He "doth not afflict willingly." Whenever God must dish out some divine correction, His heart aches. God doesn't want to rebuke us; but because of His love, He must correct us. Once He does, our reaction is important. God doesn't want to see us full of loathing and self-hatred or condemnation. Our Father simply wants us to receive His instruction and grow by it.

The importance of repentance cannot be overstated. John Bunyan warned, "If you have sinned, do not go to sleep without repentance; for the lack of repentance after one has sinned makes the heart yet harder and harder."[3]

---

3 John Bunyan, "John Bunyan," *Daily Christian Quotes*, June 27, 2018, accessed February 01, 2019, https://www.dailychristianquote.com/john-bunyan/.

There is little doubt that true repentance could be a cure-all for what ails America today. Many years ago, I learned that God cannot bless us beyond our last act of disobedience. If we wish to move forward, we must repent. Repentance causes us to go back and pick up what we left behind.

The word *repentance* means the "action of repenting; sincere regret or remorse."[4] To repent means quite literally to turn and change our behavior, and how we think about our behavior. In heaven, God will not ask us why we sinned, but He will ask us why we didn't repent.

GOD CANNOT BLESS US BEYOND OUR LAST ACT OF DISOBEDIENCE. IF WE WISH TO MOVE FORWARD, WE MUST REPENT.

I wrote down this quote many years ago in my journal, but it speaks profoundly to the importance of the subject at hand:

"Under every form and character of human life, beneath all needs and all habits, deeper than despair and more native to man than sin itself, lies the power of the heart to turn. It was this and not hope that remained at the bottom of Pandora's Box when every other gift had fled. For this is the indispensable secret of hope...and it speeds from heart to heart with a violence [that spares none]."[5]

What is the Holy Spirit saying to us today? If we will receive His rebuke, then there will be a returning or a turnaround in our lives. When we

---

4 "Repent | Definition of Repent," *Oxford Dictionaries* | English, accessed February 01, 2019, https://en.oxforddictionaries.com/definition/repent.

5 William R. Nicoll, "Jonah 3 Commentary - The Expositor's Bible Commentary," *StudyLight.org*, accessed February 01, 2019, https://www.studylight.org/commentaries/teb/jonah-3.html.

are walking in a shadow created by our own indifference and sin, all we have to do is turn! Jesus said, "Repent ye: for the kingdom of heaven is at hand" (Matthew 3:2). Everything Gideon cried out for was already within his reach, and all he had to do was turn around so he could see it.

CONTEXTUAL REPENTANCE

These are the words of Jesus:

> *Nevertheless I have somewhat against thee, because thou hast left thy first love. Remember therefore from whence thou art fallen, and repent, and do the first works; or else I will come unto thee quickly, and will remove thy candlestick out of his place, except thou repent (Revelation 2:4–5).*

It is amusing to see prominent theologians and New Testament scholars put forward wildly absurd theories as to how Jesus would respond to the modern church. Leadership gurus and seeker-sensitive strategists give further details as to how our Savior would pastor with acceptance for all, but the fact is that there's no need for speculation. While we pore over the Pauline epistles and scrutinize the correspondences from Peter, we often ignore the letters from Jesus Himself.

In the first few chapters of Revelation, we find seven letters from the Lord Jesus Christ to His church. I often refer to them as the "hidden epistles." These dynamic messages are often labeled as pure prophecy and passed over as though they were written in some coded language that only a few could ever understand. In these seven hidden epistles, we read what Jesus really thinks about our ministries, how He would deal with church discipline, and what He looks for when He attends church on Sunday morning.

In His first letter to the church at Ephesus, Jesus admonishes them to "remember therefore from whence thou are fallen, and repent and do the first works" (Revelation 2:5). This verse is often quoted by preachers in an attempt to get men and women to lay down their sin and get right with God (as we should). We tell them to remember where they lost their axe head, go back, repent, and begin to do the works they used to do for God. Although this is accurate, I believe that we have curtailed the power of repentance and limited the message.

If we continue to encourage the church to gauge the scope of their repentance solely on their own past, how can we ever expect to move forward? We've placed repentance in the wrong context. Have you noticed that modern repentance takes us back to the best that *we* can do? I don't know about you, but I need more than my own example to strive for.

Contextual repentance considers the entire panorama of history in order to truly see how far we have fallen from grace. It is interesting that Elisha's bones revived a man, while Ezekiel was able to revive the bones themselves. Either way, revival took place in a boneyard. It's as though there is something we need in what has long since been dead! Could it be that there's some glory left in the bones of other great reformers and revivalists? Could it be that if we would make contact with what has long since been dead and gone we will find new life? Gideon's cry compels every Christian to become a student of history.

If we can manage to retrace our steps, we will find the true context for our repentance and thereby discover our way back to where we lost our power. The histories of many great moves of God are readily available for all who are interested. The biographies of men like George Whitefield, John Wesley, and George Fox have already been written, and they are all waiting on the Gideons of the world to pick them up and cry, "Where are all the miracles we have heard about?"

Gideon wasn't looking for the miracles he had seen in his own past; he desired to see the greatness of God that had visited *previous* generations. It wasn't that he was ungrateful for God's protection, and it wasn't that he did not appreciate the provision he had received, but there was something deep inside Gideon that knew there was more.

Did you know that a religious mindset can make us feel as though we are selfish if we pray for "more"? I have found that it's not *what* a person prays for that makes them selfish, but it's *why* they're praying for it. If Gideon had wanted "more" so that he could become famous *that* would have been selfish. Instead, his motivation was the liberation of his people. If our hearts are in the right place, it is selfish *not* to ask for "more."

Perhaps we need to be rebuked for our selfishness, or maybe we need to be reproved for our lack of hunger. Either way, let's receive God's correction with hope, knowing that a good rebuke opens the door to true repentance. And repentance will always take us into the presence of God.

Today, we need some spiritual fathers who can offer us the rebuke we require. Pray with me that God will send these laborers into the field (Matthew 9:38), and pray that when they show up, we won't resist them, but we'll celebrate them. How can we recognize these patriarchal agents of change? Read on, and we will rediscover the power of walking in our spiritual inheritance.

CHAPTER 4: QUESTIONS FOR REFLECTION

1. The disciples didn't believe those who first told them that Jesus had risen from the dead. Why? Has there ever been a time when you didn't believe something about God that you later found to be true? How did that affect you?

2. Describe a time you remember being corrected by a parent or someone in authority in your life. How did you feel?

3. God corrects His children too. Think about an occasion when God corrected you. What did you learn from this correction?

4. We can be inspired and encouraged by reading about the revivalists of past generations. How have the stories of their experiences influenced you? What actions do they inspire you to take?

A FATHERLESS CHURCH

"Two first graders were overheard as they left Sunday school class, 'Do you really believe all that stuff about the devil?'

'No, I think it's like Santa Claus. It's really your dad.'"[1]

"Choose today whom you will serve. Would you prefer the gods your ancestors served…Or will it be the gods of the Amorites…? But as for me and my family, we will serve the LORD" (Joshua 24:15, NLT).

It has been argued, and quite persuasively, that *fatherlessness* is the primary cause of our current societal decline. Statically, 43 percent of U.S. children live in a home without their fathers, and the results are categorical:

---

1 "Devil or Santa," *Bible.org*, accessed February 01, 2019, https://bible.org/illustration/devil-or-santa.

- Ninety percent of all homeless and runaway children are from father-less homes. (U.S. Dept. of Health/Census)[2]

- Eighty-five percent of all children who show behavior disorders come from fatherless homes. (Center for Disease Control)[3]

- Seventy-one percent of all high school dropouts come from father-less homes. (National Principals Association Report)[4]

- Eighty-five percent of all youths in prison come from fatherless homes. (Fulton Co. Georgia, Texas Dept. of Correction)[5]

These statistics should in no way demean the heroic efforts of single parents across the county, but they certainly highlight the need for fathers.

Fatherlessness is damaging our nation and even our church. Paul wrote, "For though you have countless guides in Christ, you do not have many fathers" (1 Corinthians 4:15, ESV). The apostle Paul communicates to us a reality that is perhaps truer today than it was in his own time. The American church is teeming with instructors. Just turn on your TV or walk into your local Christian bookstore, and you'll hear hours of instruction and see volumes of teachings at your fingertips. This hive of instruction and abundance of teachers can be a good thing, but it could never replace the need for fathers.

Take a look at what Paul had to say about the hour we find ourselves in:

---

2 Becky Ahlberg, "U. S. Single Parent Households," *IIS Windows Server*, accessed February 01, 2019, http://lib.post.ca.gov/Publications.

3 "Statistics: The Fatherless Generation," *Index of /uploads*, January 4, 2018, accessed February 01, 2019, https://sdachurchwarwick.org/uploads.

4 Ibid.

5 Ibid.

For the time will come when they will not endure sound doctrine;
but after their own lusts shall they heap to themselves teachers,
having itching ears; and they shall turn away their ears from
the truth, and shall be turned unto fables (2 Timothy 4:3–4).

It appears that Paul is conflating an abundance of teachers with a back-slidden church. Why? The office of the teacher plays a vital role in the fivefold ministry that God has given to the church for the perfecting of the saints, and for the work of the ministry. What's the difference between an instructor and a father? Why do those with itching ears seek to heap up teachers, rather than cling to fathers? Why is there such a shortage of father figures in the American church?

The reason we find ourselves in this predicament may be surprising: freedom! The Bible warns that we shouldn't allow our blessing to become our curse; in this case, it seems that we may have stepped over that line just a tad. With freedom comes an abundance of choices. Thank God we have such freedoms in our nation.

Imagine what would happen if kids had the freedom to choose their parents or if students were allowed to choose their teachers? Faced with such a choice, would a teenager choose the parent or teacher who demanded excellence from them, or would they choose the one who allowed them to do whatever they wanted?

Human nature dictates that people will follow the path of least resistance, so when presented with a choice between a father and a teacher, many will choose the latter. Why? Teachers give you information, while fathers give you discipline. Teachers inspire, while fathers demand accountability.

Teachers talk *about* God, but fathers speak *for* God. Is it any wonder Paul says that mankind will "heap to themselves teachers" (2 Timothy 4:3)? Due to the plethora of teachers and instructors now available to the average Christian, the overwhelming current of the culture demands that pastors with fatherly tendencies ease up, pull back, and demand less in order to compete.

TEACHERS TALK ABOUT GOD, BUT FATHERS SPEAK FOR GOD.

Many single parents struggle with this very issue. Getting our children to clean their rooms, keep their grades up, and do their chores can be a daunting task, but it's far worse when they go away on the weekends to a place that demands nothing of them. While they're away—at the other parent's home—sometimes there's no curfew, they can play all the video games they want, and they don't have to clean anything. After being presented with such an easy alternative, these children now think the responsible parent is *unreasonable* and will, in a huff, declare their desire to live elsewhere.

This is what true fathers in the body of Christ now must deal with on a daily basis. Our spiritual fathers are trying to prepare us for life, and life eternal, while others are just trying to get our attention. Teachers will use any means necessary to pique our interest, while fathers will simply demand it. A popular church growth strategy today is to preach about change but *never* demand it—and it is working. People love to feel like they're being challenged, as long as they are never really required to change.

THE CHILDREN'S MINISTRY GENERATION

One of the greatest innovations of the last century was children's ministry. The idea of having a separate service just for children was, in some ways, revolutionary. Done well, it can raise up warriors for the kingdom of God. However, if it becomes a babysitting service meant to entertain—with a little Bible lesson thrown in—it can be disastrous.

For hundreds of years, children were forced to sit quietly in the service with their parents, respect the minister, and listen to the Word of God whether they understood it or not. This produced a discipline rarely seen today.

Once they were taken out of the adult service, they were presented with puppets, light shows, skits, and a never-ending array of props meant to keep their attention. These things in and of themselves can be good; and can make for an amazing children's ministry. But if this is all our children know they will never become acclimated to adult church.

George Barna conducted a survey of self-pronounced Christians, and here's what he found out about their knowledge of the Bible. Keep in mind these are Christians!

- Forty-eight percent could not name the four Gospels.

- Fifty-two percent could not identify more than two or three of Jesus' disciples.

- Sixty percent of American Christians can't name even five of the Ten Commandments.

- Sixty-one percent of American Christians think the Sermon on the Mount was preached by Billy Graham.

- Seventy-one percent of American Christians think "God helps those who help themselves" is a Bible verse. (Actually Benjamin Franklin wrote that.)[6]

George Barna said, "Americans revere the Bible, but by and large, they don't know what it says. And because they don't know it, they have become a nation of biblical illiterates."[7]

Today, many Christians do not have a clear idea about what the role of the church should be or what its purpose actually is. The focus is on "us" in the church, not those we should be trying to reach with the message of the gospel.

This "Children's Church Generation" is all grown up now and they want to be entertained. No, they don't just want it; they demand it! The thought of an old statesman of the faith systematically outlining doctrine bores them, and the moving of the Holy Spirit scares them. "Where are the light shows, the skits, and the props we're accustomed to?" they cry. "Don't make us uncomfortable, or we'll find another show down the road."

I'm not saying we should abolish children's ministry, but it does help to know why we are where we are. We now have an entire generation that demands *accommodation* and shuns *confrontation*. In this environment, it's easy for pastors to get caught unawares, especially if they themselves were raised in it.

How can we fix it? I believe we can begin by becoming aware of how we

---

6 Timothy Smith, "George Barna Wrote The State Of The Church In...," *Sermon Central*, January 01, 2005, accessed February 01, 2019, https://www.sermoncentral.com/sermon-illustrations/19353/bible-study-by-timothy-smith?ref=TextIllustrationSerps.
7 Ibid.

define success in the American church. Today, success in church is primarily defined by one thing: attendance. The bigger our church is, the more successful we are deemed to be. The glamour of a relatively new phenomena called the megachurch has blinded us to the reality that the average church size in America is still somewhere between 50–75 people (as it has been throughout history).

In an age where we're constantly lowering our standards, using attendance and so-called conversions to gauge our success would be like lowering educational standards and then bragging about higher test scores. This is not just for the consideration of pastors and church leaders either. The average Christian needs a means of gauging their success as well.

If we can't use attendance as a gauge for success, what can we use? I would submit to you that spiritual proficiency would be a good place to set a standard. I know that this may seem revolutionary, but what if the goal of the pastor was to ensure that the members were actually trained to effectively minister the gospel?

Here are a few questions ministries could use to measure the spiritual proficiency of their church:

- How many of your members understand and can explain the fundamental doctrines of the church as outlined in Hebrews 6 (repentance, faith, baptisms, laying on of hands, resurrection, and eternal judgment)?

- How many of your members know how to cast out a devil, lay hands on the sick, and win the lost?

- How many of your members understand and can explain the Holy Spirit and His gifts?

- If there's a call to prayer, how many of your members can enter into intercession?

These are relatively simple questions; yet, somehow they uproot our current understanding of success in the body of Christ. We may have thousands in our Sunday service, but how many are actually becoming effective ministers of the gospel?

ACCOMMODATION HAS BECOME THE BANDIT OF THE MODERN CHURCH.

A reexamination of what church is about is desperately needed. Historically and biblically, the church was created to equip believers to *reach* the world; yet now we've designed our services to *appeal* to the world. Accommodation has become the bandit of the modern church. We must come to grips with the reality that we cannot seriously equip the saints, while catering to "seekers" at the same time. Perhaps if we design our services to train believers and raise up a generation of Gideons we'll see more sinners saved.

CHAPTER 5: QUESTIONS FOR REFLECTION

1. How has the absence of a father figure affected you, or someone you know? What can you do about changing the influence this has had on you, or someone close to you?

2. "Fathers demand accountability." What does this mean? Have you ever been made accountable by an authority figure in your life? Have you ever been the one to hold someone else accountable? Describe this experience.

3. There are five questions listed that George Barna used in a survey of Christians about their Bible knowledge. How many of these would you have been able to answer correctly?

4. What does the term *spiritual proficiency* mean to you? How would you measure it?

Chapter 6

YOU'VE GOT TOO MANY

"The LORD said to Gideon, You have too many people"
(Judges 7:2, HCSB).

"History shows clearly enough that true spirituality has never at any time been the possession of the masses. In any given period since the fall of the human race, only a few persons ever discerned the right way or walked in God's law. God's truth has never been popular. Wherever Christianity becomes popular, it is not on its way to die—it has already died. Popular Judaism slew the prophets and crucified Christ. Popular Christianity killed the Reformers, jailed the Quakers, and drove John Wesley into the streets. When it comes to religion, the crowds are always wrong"—A.W. Tozer[1]

---

1 A. W. Tozer, "Tozer Devotional | When Fish Catch the Fisherman," *The Alliance*, April 09, 2016, accessed February 02, 2019, https://www.cmalliance.org/devotions/tozer?id=411.

Hold on to your pearls, because what you're about to read could send today's church growth gurus, along with their acolytes, into cardiac arrest. However, if we open up our spirits and our minds, we may just hear God saying something that is as liberating as it is true.

Two pastors were catching up one day on how their churches were doing. One pastor said, "We're doing great! When I got here, there were only forty people. After implementing a few new programs, we now have four hundred."

The other pastor said, "That's funny, because when I got to my church we had about one hundred. After years of just preaching the old-fashioned gospel, I've got them down to ten."[2]

Where did we get the idea that the real gospel draws a crowd? If we can barely get people to stand in line for a flavored coffee at the mall, how in the world are we supposed to get them to line up for the cross of Christ? It is certainly true that Jesus offers "life, and life more abundantly," but His life is only accessible through death. That's quite an entrance fee! It takes real fathers to tell us this.

The real gospel is not as stylish, comforting, and cool as we'd like to think. Churches often justify their drive for success by citing the thousands that followed Jesus, and the thousands that were born again on the day of Pentecost. *But,* how many of the multitudes actually accompanied these leaders to jail, or even to the cross? We've confused spectators for real Spirit-filled believers and partisans for Pentecostals. Just because someone is a sympathizer doesn't mean they're serious about the kingdom of God.

---

2 Source unknown.

The truth is that people—especially masses already susceptible to group-think—are easily moved by passion but the perils of discipleship soon separate the wheat from the chaff. Real, radical discipleship demands more than attending an entertaining service once a week. This is an important fact that many are overlooking in their Black Friday dash for church growth.

ISN'T GROWTH GOOD?

Isn't growth good? The answer to this question depends on our definition of growth and success. Another survey by the Barna Research Institute asked pastors how they define success. The pastors' responses ranged from attendance and staff to square footage of their buildings. You can almost smell the stench of pop culture on our church leadership.[3]

"Bigger is better! Supersize me!" We may not build golden calves to show our selfish and limited revelation of God anymore, but we do build monuments, empires, and enormous amounts of debt in an attempt to show the world our God.

They had a similar mindset in Jesus' day concerning their great religious accomplishments, but He said, "Not one stone will be left on top of another" (Matthew 24:2, NLT). How are we any different?

I am more convinced than ever that the desperate drive to grow the church will inevitably destroy it instead. Dietrich Bonhoeffer said:

"The person who loves their dream of community will destroy commu-

---

3 John Souter, "Why Are Our Pastors Not Preaching the Truth?" *When to Disobey Authority*, accessed February 02, 2019, http://freshlightsource.com/believers/whypastorsnottellingtruth. html.

nity, even if their intentions are ever so earnest, but the person who loves those around them will create community."[4]

What has this church growth madness done to the average minister? The desire for this kind of superficial growth often heightens the pressure to lower the standard. Masses were no miracle to Jesus, nor to the apostles. Anyone can draw a crowd.

THE TRUE TEST OF ONE'S MINISTRY IS NOT HOW MANY SHOW UP, BUT HOW MANY ARE SIFTED OUT.

The true test of one's ministry is not how many show up, but how many are sifted out. The New Testament church demanded holiness, and they would publicly shame those who refused to repent. Today, preachers feel like they're really putting it on the line if they preach a sermon on sin, but they would never address it directly because that would make people uncomfortable.

The New Testament church demanded commitment and discipline, even unto death. Today, we request that our members attend a catered life group—if they have time in their busy schedules. The desire for such perceived success pushes us to put on the facade of perceived success. However, God is much more concerned about protecting His church from apostasy than He is in increasing attendance.

The desire for this kind of growth increases the need to be competitive.

4 Dietrich Bonhoeffer, "A Quote from Life Together: The Classic Exploration of Christian Community," *Goodreads*, accessed February 02, 2019, https://www.goodreads.com/quotes/911415-the-person-who-loves-their-dream-of-community-will-destroy.

I've had pastors admit to me that they wouldn't invite a certain minister to their church because they were afraid that their members would leave to join that guest minister's church. Of course, we will never admit to ourselves that these petty feelings exist, so we come up with a variety of reasons to justify our envy of other ministers or their ministries. Everyone loves to talk about "unity" until someone leaves their church to attend another. The search for growth causes us to view our real family in Christ as a rival that must be beaten, instead of a united body that must be maintained and protected.

Finally, the desire for growth blinds us from being able to distinguish between perceived success and real success. Everyone will say, "it's not about numbers" because that's the thing to say, but in their hearts it's not true. Don't believe me? Find one national Christian conference that has an eighty-year-old pastor of a seventy-five-member church as its keynote speaker. He's been preaching for sixty years, but we'd rather hear from some young hipster who has 5,000 in his services on any given Sunday.

We can't just point our finger at those who put on these conferences. What about those who attend?

"They must be doing something right. Look at all the people they have in their ministry!" They may certainly be doing something right, but the number of people being entertained is no way to determine success. If numbers equaled success in the kingdom, Beyoncé would be one of the twenty-four elders!

Here's the big lie that gets thrown around to justify doctrinal and spiritual error: "Well, at least people are getting saved!" That's like defending a negligent and abusive parent by saying, "Well, at least they're having more kids!" We're willing to endure a host of errors as long as we think the Great Commission is being fulfilled—but is it? We mask our shallow need for growth by calling it "a passion for evangelism." What about the Great Commission? Isn't there an inherent command to grow in the Great Commission? Let's look at it again:

> Go ye into all the world, and preach the gospel to every creature" (Mark 16:15).

> Go ye therefore, and teach all nations, baptizing them in the name of the Father, and of the Son, and of the Holy Ghost: teaching them to observe all things whatsoever I have commanded you: and, lo, I am with you always, even unto the end of the world. Amen (Matthew 28:19–20).

The Great Commission is simple: "Preach the gospel." The Great Commission is not about "saving souls" or "getting crowds." This may seem like a distinction without a difference, but I assure you that the difference is as far as the east is from the west. If the mission is to "win souls," then we will do whatever is necessary to reach as many as we can; we will even alter the message. However, if the mission is to "preach the gospel," then we must do whatever is necessary to preserve the integrity of the message—no matter how society reacts to it.

Acceptance is an intoxicant, and the modern church needs an intervention. It's time we get back to the mission of the Great Commission and realize that the drive for success is a pollutant in the river of life.

The good news is that if we don't have to spend so much time growing the church, we can focus on ministering to our family in the body of Christ. This will, no doubt, be a difficult transition for many. I would recommend turning off Christian TV, fasting most major conferences, and throwing away those church strategy books just for a little while. After a period of seeing nothing but our people and the Word of God, we'll forget that there's a race for success going on outside our walls! We will discover a contentment that is truly transforming.

PASTOR-IZATION

In the 1850s, a man named Louis Pasteur discovered that bacteria could be killed by heat. Pasteur later invented a heat treatment to kill harmful bacteria, and this process has become known as *pasteurization*. Pasteurization is the application of extreme heat to kill bacteria and extend the shelf life in food.

IT MAY BE TIME TO START OVER WITH NOTHING BUT AN EMPTY ROOM, THE WORD OF GOD, AND A SPIRITUAL FATHER.

In the church today, we need some pastors to take their rightful place as fathers in the faith and begin to apply some heat to our lives. This kind of "pastor-ization" will help eliminate false doctrine, narrow the Enemy's foothold, and ensure our success in the family of God. The modern church service has become so deformed—and we've grown so spoiled—that it may be time to start over with nothing but an empty room, the Word of God, and a spiritual father. It's time for the church to come out of the gutter, avoid the ditches, and get back in the trenches. Let's pray for our pastors to continue to grow in wisdom and in boldness as we grow in meekness and Sonship.

> *Obey your spiritual leaders, and do what they say. Their work is to watch over your souls, and they are accountable to God. Give them reason to do this with joy and not with sorrow. That would certainly not be for your benefit (Hebrews 13:17, NLT).*

Gideon's cry is one that honors the leadership we have in our present while reaching for the tried and tested principles of the past. We cannot receive from the fathers of the faith of previous generations until we honor the ones we have now. Where is the power? It's often found in true Sonship and submission to spiritual authority.

CHAPTER 6: QUESTIONS FOR REFLECTION

1. "His life is only accessible through death." What does this mean to you? What kind of *death* is required to live this Christian life?

2. "The desire for…superficial growth often heightens the pressure to lower the standard." In what ways have standards been lowered in the modern church?

3. "Acceptance is an intoxicant." How has the need for acceptance affected you, or the way you serve as a church member?

4. What does the Great Commission mean to you?

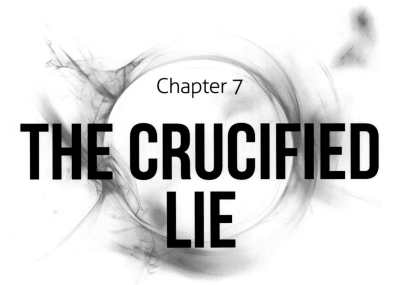

Chapter 7

THE CRUCIFIED LIE

"Do your worst, I am a Christian. Christ is my help and supporter, and thus armed I will never serve your gods nor do I fear your authority or that of your master, the Emperor. Commence your torments as soon as you please, and make use of every means that your malignity can invent, and you shall find in the end that I am not to be shaken from my resolution."
—Andronicus, A.D. 290[1]

"Fear none of those things which thou shalt suffer: behold, the devil shall cast some of you into prison, that ye may be tried; and ye shall have tribulation ten days: be thou faithful unto death, and I will give thee a crown of life" (Revelation 2:10).

---

1 Pat Cook, "Praying for the Persecuted," Sermon Central, November 15, 2004, accessed February 04, 2019, https://www.sermoncentral.com/sermons/praying-for-the-persecuted-pat-cook-sermon-on-endurance-73779?ref=SermonSerps.

Gideon's cry is one that disassociates personal cost from the equation when seeking divine power. The contemporary church has been told to "take up [the] cross" (Matthew 16:24); but since for many their only point of reference for a cross is a necklace or a bumper sticker, they have no idea what that means. The modern Christian thinks taking up the cross means not eating chocolate for the forty days of Lent or tolerating an annoying coworker.

The cross represents an execution. Real resurrection power can only come from fortitude in the face of execution. Here is one example of a fearless saint as he faced certain martyrdom:

"Polycarp was a disciple of the Apostle John and an early church leader whose life ended when he refused to betray his Lord. Asked one last time to disavow his Christ, the old man replied, 'Eighty and six years have I served Him, and He has done me no wrong. How can I speak evil of my King who saved me?' Here is his martyr's prayer, as recorded by the historian Eusebius.

"'Father of Your beloved and blessed Son Jesus Christ, through whom we have received the knowledge of You, I bless You that You have counted me worthy of this day and hour, that I might be in the number of the martyrs. Among these may I be received before You today in a rich and acceptable sacrifice, as You have beforehand prepared and revealed. Wherefore I also praise You also for everything; I bless You; I glorify You, through the eternal High Priest Jesus Christ, Your beloved Son, through whom, with Him, in the Holy Spirit, be glory unto You both now and for the ages to come. Amen.'

Eusebius adds: "When he had offered up his amen and had finished his prayer, the firemen lighted the fire.'"[2]

Instead of a crucified *life*, we've been sold a crucified *lie*. We're told that we can take up our cross by giving a little extra in the offering or going to more than one service a week at our church. Here's a revelation: Jesus didn't crucify Himself, and neither can we! The truth is this: If we are to follow Jesus' example, we cannot take up our cross and follow Him until our devotion to God makes people so uncomfortable that *they* rally to crucify us.

> ## INSTEAD OF A CRUCIFIED LIFE, WE'VE BEEN SOLD A CRUCIFIED LIE.

RECOVERING THE REMNANT

In an age when everyone wants to be validated, understood, and justified in the eyes of their peers, God is looking for some Gideons who aren't going to run from their own personal firing squad.

> *And in that day there shall be a root of Jesse, which shall stand for an ensign of the people; to it shall the Gentiles seek: and his rest shall be glorious. And it shall come to pass in that day, that the Lord shall set his hand again the second time to recover the remnant of his people (Isaiah 11:10–11).*

---

2 Eusebius, "Polycarp's Prayer," *Bible.org*, accessed February 02, 2019, https://bible.org/illustration/polycarps-prayer, quoted in Closer Walk, July 1988, 22.

In different periods of history, the church—by divine revelation—has placed emphasis on different truths. At one time, it will be on global missions or worship, and at another it will be on healing or ecumenicalism. It has been that way since its inception on the day of Pentecost, and it is no different in our own time. As we enter into a new season in church history, the Holy Spirit is calling the church to major on its own renewal. After all, before we can move forward, we must be honest about where we are.

Abraham Lincoln said, "If we could first know where we are, and whither we are tending, we could better judge what to do and how to do it."[3]

This is a vital truth that we must take to heart as we step into a new mission field. Optimism has its place; but if we desire to move forward, *realism* is the only feasible starting point. In an effort to "be real," I want to state this truth as emphatically as I can: Until we understand where we really are, we will never be able to advance.

COMMITTED CHRISTIANS AND BELIEVING BELIEVERS ARE A MINORITY

The contemporary weakness of the church stems in part from a miscalculation of its own strength and acceptance. When reading the New Testament, it doesn't take long to realize that part of the power of the early church rose from the clear recognition that it was by no means conventional or popular. The call to take the gospel around the world was prefaced by the clear recognition that opposition was to be expected.

---

3 Abraham Lincoln, "House Divided Speech," *National Parks Service*, accessed February 02, 2019, https://www.nps.gov/liho/learn/historyculture/housedivided.htm, quoted from M. E. Neely, *The Abraham Lincoln Encyclopedia* (New York: McGraw-Hill Book Company, 1982).

Paul confessed confidently that "a wide door for effective work has opened to me, and there are many adversaries" (1 Corinthians 16:9, ESV). At that time, Christians were surrounded by uncompromising pagans and religious zealots who were contemptuous at best; *but since opposition was expected*, the early Christians prepared themselves for it spiritually, mentally, emotionally, and even physically.

Today, we're dazzled by new and exciting life groups that promise to teach us how to witness to others about our faith *without offense!* We've mastered the art of camouflage, and we're basking in the warmth of cultural acceptance. In many ways, contemporary Christians are less fortunate than our first-century counterparts because of this perceived acceptance. It is a delusion.

There is no doubt that our nation has been baptized in "Christianese"— with an abundance of Christian music, TV, movies, T-shirts, necklaces, and bumper stickers. If we believe this means we still hold a lion's share of cultural influence, we're mistaken. Looks can be deceiving, especially in something as important as this.

Just look at Europe, where the landscape is filled with beautiful churches and cathedrals but has little to no Christian influence today. The external evidences of a religion may go on for a long time after the power of that religion to influence the masses has disappeared. People will still get married and buried via the church—long after prayer and other real Christian disciplines have passed away.

The fact is that "believing" believers are a minority who are just as hard to find in church on Sunday as they are in a bar on Saturday. This is a fact well-hidden if you merely judge by name only. Church attendance is sky-rocketing, but it seems that what people are embracing—by and large—is not true committed Christianity, but vague religiosity.

The apostle's words to the Athenians are just as suitable *today*: "I perceive that in every way you are very religious." (Acts 17:22, ESV). Don't get me wrong: Being a minority is not a problem, and it does not hinder our ability to influence our nation. However, refusing to acknowledge our minority status provides misguided expectations as unsuspecting believers attempt to fulfill the call of God on their lives. We cannot be rightly prepared for what's coming if we do not understand the intensity of the opposition to *real* Christianity.

SELFISHNESS ALWAYS TURNS SPIRITUALITY INTO A VERY PRIVATE MATTER.

This new watered-down version of Christianity preaches the doctrine of personal spirituality and worn-out hedonism that rejects accountability and discipline. They scoff at holiness, claiming freedom from such antiquated ideas. The person whose primary focus is his own pleasure and liberty will logically become anti-church because he is doomed to see church and its membership—with all its responsibilities—as something that limits his own personal freedom. Selfishness always turns spirituality into a very private matter.

Inevitably, some will say, "It is nobody else's business. It's between me and God." No! Our Christianity is between us and our church, which is the body of Christ. We cannot do anything in a vacuum. Everything we do directly affects the body of which we are a part.

According to Jesus, freedom is not acquired automatically.

Then said Jesus to those Jews which believed on him, If ye continue in my word, then are ye my disciples indeed; and ye shall know the truth, and the truth shall make you free (John 8:31–32).

Participation and commitment to the life of a "disciplined one" is the price of that freedom. The current "easy-believism" trend is a far cry from what the cross provided. This buffet style of religion is picking up steam, and it will continue to grow in acceptance, feeding the lie that real Christianity is growing when in reality it is just as rejected now as it was 2,000 years ago.

The early church prospered because it was willing to be counted worthy of persecution. We must ask ourselves, "Are we willing to embrace the scandal of real Christianity?" We can no longer maintain a nominal membership that costs us nothing in our churches and expect to please God. We will be far more effective if we understand the sacrifice that is expected and realize that the gospel will never be accepted by the majority in this life.

What we need today is a true conversion, not of the individual but of the church itself! Christians have been scattered, but unlike the ones whom God redeemed from Egypt, the confrontation of one Pharaoh will not be enough. We are like those in the Book of Isaiah who have been scattered into various forms of captivity. God's desire is to recover the remnant, already quoted in Isaiah 11.

And it shall come to pass in that day, that the LORD shall set his hand again the second time to recover the remnant of his people (Isaiah 11:11).

It's time to preach the gospel to the church so that God's remnant can be restored, and so that we can carry this glorious gospel to the world. We must humble ourselves or be humiliated. No more stalling! It's time to submit everything to His Lordship.

Are we ready to submit to a plan for our lives that is so supernatural that it will *require* the miraculous just to stand against the opposition we will face? Like the disciples in Acts 4, are we ready to preach a message so radical that it will have us pleading for heavenly boldness? Leonard Ravenhill said, "The world out there is not waiting for a new definition of Christianity; it's waiting for a new *demonstration* of Christianity."[4]

A WORD TO PREACHERS AND THOSE WHO PRAY FOR THEM

We are in need of some fearless men and women who will declare the Word of God with passion and power. "The Rev. Dr. Robert South, while preaching one day in 1689, looked up from his notes to observe that his entire congregation was fast asleep—including the King! Appropriately mortified by this discovery, he interrupted his sermon to call out, 'Lord Lauderdale, rouse yourself. You snore so loudly that you will wake the King.'"[5]

---

4 Leonard Ravenhill, "The World out There Is Not Waiting for a New Definition of Christianity; It's Waiting for a New Demonstration of Christi...," *Leonard Ravenhill Quote*: accessed February 02, 2019, https://quotefancy.com/quote/852277/Leonard-Ravenhill-The-world-out-there-is-not-waiting-for-a-new-definition-of-Christianity

5 "Boring Sermon," *Bible.org*, accessed February 02, 2019, https://bible.org/illustration/boring-sermon.

Charles Haddon Spurgeon instructed his Bible students to "preach not calmly and quietly as though you were asleep, but preach with fire and pathos and passion."[6] In the face of certain disapproval and high-tech persecution, preachers need to be encouraged to preach again.

Throughout the years, I've had the unique opportunity to work with ministers around the globe. It's been a great honor to work with these ambassadors, and over time I've developed a real passion for preachers. I understand their labor, and I identify with their struggles.

As our culture changes, the provincial practice of the preacher marches on, unaffected by societal or political confusion. This above all things can keep the head of the preacher on a swivel as society clamors for truth one minute and demands their head on a platter the next.

Today, preaching has become passé, and the call to compromise is as enticing as ever. This is why we must pray for our preachers while encouraging them in their work. Let them know that you support their mission as they declare the truth, unvarnished by the current cultural climate. It is not through the cleverness of teaching that God has promised to rescue our generation, but by the foolishness of preaching.

Leonard Ravenhill said, "If Jesus had preached the same message that ministers preach today, He would never have been crucified."[7]

In an effort to explain the lack of soul-hot preaching, there are those mas-

---

6 Charles Haddon Spurgeon, "Charles Spurgeon Quotes About Preaching," *A-Z Quotes*, accessed February 02, 2019, https://www.azquotes.com/author/13978-Charles_Spurgeon/tag/preaching, quoted from Charles H. Spurgeon, *The Two Wesleys On John and Charles Wesley* (Eugene, OR: Wipf & Stock Pub, 2014).

7 Leonard Ravenhill, "Leonard Ravenhill Quote," *A-Z Quotes*, accessed February 02, 2019, https://www.azquotes.com/quote/673525.

ters of marketing that say that the message never changes, but the methods do. Although I understand their heart and believe in their mission to keep the church "up on the times," the sad reality is that *the method never changes*. God has always delivered His message through the preaching of the gospel, and He always will. No amount of marketing can replace a declared Word that has been saturated in prayer and delivered in power. Preaching has the inherent power to move men and women to action:

> **NO AMOUNT OF MARKETING CAN REPLACE A DECLARED WORD THAT HAS BEEN SATURATED IN PRAYER AND DELIVERED IN POWER.**

"The preacher should…see preaching much more as a declaration of war, a conflict in which well-disciplined words march as to war to bring the hearers to surrender to Jesus Christ. We need to use the pulpit as a battle station." —C.J. Miller[8]

The late B.H. Clendennen declared: "It is impossible to overestimate the importance of the preacher. A dying church will downgrade the preacher and his preaching. Theatrics replace preaching, counseling replaces deliverance. Bible colleges put more emphasis on music and musicians than on preaching and preachers…As the voice of God he is only to speak what he is told. He has letters from the King of Kings. Samuel was the medium on which God's heart broke into language, and through which the infinite purpose of God caused itself to be heard in all the indignation proper to its outrage."[9]

8 C. J. Miller, "Quotes on Ministry in the Church," *Keith Malcomson*, accessed February 02, 2019, https://keithmalcomson.weebly.com/quotes-on-ministry-in-the-church.html.

9 B. H. Clendennen, "The Preacher as a Man of God," *The New Cruse*, accessed February 04, 2019, http://www.thenewcruse.pentecostalpioneers.org/preachermanofgod.html.

The words of a preacher, delivered with passion and a spirit of no compromise, can have an incalculable effect on those who hear them:

"Works of stone will crumble, time will eat up the pyramids, but the work of the preacher will be glorious when the world shall be burned up. The preacher shall lead the way."[10]

Preachers, it's time to stoke the fires that birthed us, because when we're born in the fire, we can't live in the smoke. Love doesn't require accommodation; neither does compassion require compromise. Love requires unction, and compassion compels heralds to cry loud and spare not. Before we take our pulpits, let's read the following lines in our secret place and allow them to pierce our souls and stir our spirits:

The Cry of a Distressed Soul

O Preacher, holy man, hear my heart weeping;
I long to stand and shout my protests:
Where is your power?
And where is your message?
Where is the Gospel of mercy and love?
Your words are nothingness!
Nothingness! Nothingness!
We who have come to listen are betrayed.

Servant of God, I am bitter and desolate.
What do I care for perfection of phrase?
Cursed be you humor, your praise, your diction.
See how my soul turns to ashes within me.

---

10 Ibid.

You who have vowed to declare your Redeemer,

Give me the words that would save!

Written by Margaret Chaplin Anderson[11]

I am standing in faith with you, Preacher. Go, and declare all that God has placed in your heart. Gideon's cry is just that…a cry! There are those who mistakenly think that Jesus was a passive teacher who never raised His voice. This couldn't be further from the truth. Isaiah 58:1 plainly says, "Cry aloud, spare not, lift up thy voice like a trumpet." Wasn't our Lord Jesus Christ this very Word made flesh? He most certainly cried and shouted and wept. But, it's not the volume that matters as much as where the cry is coming from. Gideon's cry is like fire shut up in the bones (Jeremiah 20:9).

There is hope for those who have lost their passion. Smith Wigglesworth said, "The man who is a preacher, if he has lost the unction, will be well repaid if he will repent and get right with God and get the unction back."[12]

The Day of Pentecost, in Acts 2, certainly meant *power* to the disciples, but it also meant *prison* to them. Yet, they were happy to endure the persecution if it meant getting an answer to the question, "Where is the power?" Whether we're preachers or pew-sitters, it's time to become the remnant with a fire in our hearts and a two-edged sword in our mouths. It may not be popular, but it will produce power and bring about a divine encounter.

11 Margaret Chaplin Anderson, quoted in Leonard Ravenhill, *Revival God's Way: A Message for the Church* (Minneapolis, MN: Bethany House, 2006).

12 Smith Wigglesworth, "The Active Life of the Spirit-filled Believer," Smith Wigglesworth | Bibliography | *Pensketches* | Brixton to Albert Hall, accessed February 02, 2019, http://www.smithwigglesworth.com/sermons/misc4.htm,quoted from Anna C. Reiff, ed., "The Active Life of the Spirit-filled Believer," *Latter Rain Evangel*, February 1923.

The crucified lie tells us that we can be crucified with Christ and still keep parts of our own personality and old life alive. Paul, on the other hand—with Gideon's cry in his heart—said, "I die daily" (1 Corinthians 15:31). Here is the embodiment of the declaration that the apostle Paul made of his life and his mission:

> *I am crucified with Christ: nevertheless* **I live***; yet not I,* **but Christ** *liveth in me: and the life which I now live in the flesh I live by the faith of the Son of God, who loved me, and gave himself for me (Galatians 2:20, emphasis added).*

CHAPTER 7: QUESTIONS FOR REFLECTION

1. What does "taking up the cross" mean to you? How does this translate into your everyday life and actions?

2. Leonard Ravenhill said, "The world out there is not waiting for a new definition of Christianity; it's waiting for a new demonstration of Christianity." How do you define Christianity in your life? How do you demonstrate that Christianity?

3. What form of opposition have you had to endure because you are a Christian? How did you respond to this opposition?

4. Think of a time when a message you heard preached motivated you to action. What was it that prompted you to act, and what action did you take?

Chapter 8

THE NEW MISSION FIELD

"The Church is not a soup kitchen for the devil's kids."
—Lester Sumrall[1]

"Is it time for you yourselves to dwell in your paneled houses, while this house lies in ruins?" (Haggai 1:4, ESV).

"In the 1830s, the shores of Hawaii were visited by a titan of the faith. His name was Titus Coan, and thousands gathered wherever he was to hear the Word of God. They didn't come to hear a nice motivational message. They came to hear what they already knew in their hearts—that they were sinners in need of a Savior. The convicting power of God was so strong in these meetings that Mr. Coan would have to stop preaching because of

---

1 Lester Sumrall, "Interview with Lester Sumrall," interview by Paul Crouch and Jan Crouch, *TBN*, November 27, 1984.

the volume of the multitudes crying out for mercy and wailing in repentance. Thousands would be slain in the Spirit as they cried out for God's forgiveness. Some would scream, 'The two-edged sword is cutting me to pieces!' Others who came to scoff ended up crying out, 'What must I do to be saved?' Sins were confessed, renounced and forgiven and Titus Coan himself baptized nearly twelve thousand people."[2]

The Word of God is a sword. Should it surprise us that it cuts? The Word of God is a fire. Should it shock us that it burns? To have Gideon's cry in our hearts is to be willing to endure the cut of the sword because we know that whatever it exposes, it heals. This chapter may cut us a little, but we will find relief in its truth.

There is an old stereotype that doctors don't get sick. This is obviously false. However, there is another stereotype about doctors that I would more readily accept, which states that doctors make the worst patients. It would be putting it mildly to say that it is tough to treat someone who thinks they already know it all.

Recently, I had the opportunity to interview a group of teenagers. Most of them had been raised in church their entire lives and had attended youth groups every week as long as they could remember. My question was simple: "What is the Great Commission?" After a long, uncomfortable pause, I was startled as I stared into blank faces. No one had an answer. I began to ask Christian adults the same question, and I received the same response.

The Great Commission is the call of every blood-bought believer. It defines who we are, doesn't it? The reality is that God has placed a divine

---

2 Oswald J. Smith, *The Revival We Need* (Shoals, IN: First Kingsley Press, 2012).

"Go!" within His church. God has sent us to reach many different people groups, from many different backgrounds. He has sent us to the Russian, the Asian, the African, the European, and the Arab. Our loving Creator has sent us to the Buddhist, the Taoist, the Hindus, the Muslims, and the atheists.

We have been called to *go*, and through the centuries we have gone. Regardless of the threat of persecution, shame, and ostracism, the soldiers of the cross have marched with dogged determination to lift up the blood-stained banner of Jesus Christ and bring the light of the gospel to the darkest recesses of the known world.

Many people groups and faiths have arisen during that time whose customs and practices boggle the mind, but there has always been a remnant who allowed themselves to become contrarians to a culture in need of clarity. These men and women of faith stood against Hitler and his Reich, against the evils of slavery, and against the tyranny of despotic governments. They have held their own when faced with the unreasoning views of a radical Islam and have stood face to face confronting abortion providers and witch doctors alike.

THERE HAS ALWAYS BEEN A REMNANT WHO ALLOWED THEMSELVES TO BECOME CONTRARIANS TO A CULTURE IN NEED OF CLARITY.

These were men and women of whom the world was not worthy; and they gladly laid down their lives to take the gospel where it was needed most. It seems, though, that these heroes of the faith have become relics of the past. By the mid-twentieth century, it looked as though the church had become weary and was beginning to turn inward. This introspection turned into selfishness, and just ten years ago you couldn't find many churches or pastors who had that divine "Go" burning in their hearts. But even though things are changing rapidly, especially since evangelism is becoming the church-growth strategy of the day, we're still in need of a revival.

As we stand on the edge of the greatest fulfillment of prophecy ever witnessed, in these last days, God is calling on us to face a new menace. There is a new threat rising that can cause great damage to the church. Only the brave and the bold will have the stomach to face it. This is what I'm calling the "new mission field."

This "new mission field" is wrapped in a protective cocoon by this culture and carefully guarded by Satan himself, as he slowly eats away at their souls. He's done a convincing job:

- Six out of ten do not believe that Satan is even real.[3]

- More than half say there is no absolute truth.[4]

- One third believe abortion should be legal.[5]

- Nearly half believe that marriage should be redefined.[6]

---

3 "Most American Christians Do Not Believe That Satan or the Holy Spirit Exist," *Barna Group*, accessed February 02, 2019, https://www.barna.com/research/most-american.

4 "The End of Absolutes: America's New Moral Code," *Barna Group*, May 25, 2016, accessed February 02, 2019, https://www.barna.com/research/the-end-of-absolutes-americas-new-moral-code/.

5 "Religion in America: U.S. Religious Data, Demographics and Statistics," *Pew Research Center's Religion & Public Life Project*, May 11, 2015, accessed February 02, 2019, http://www.pewforum.org/religious-landscape-study/views-about-abortion.

6 Ibid.

- One out of five have a biblical worldview.[7]

Names matter. In order to reach this group, topple its faulty ideology, and present the gospel to them, we must define them. They have been traditionally known as "Christians." Some may refer to them as "the church," but I prefer to simply call them the "new mission field." Make no mistake: they are as much a stranger to the gospel as the atheist and as much an alien to the promises of God as an agnostic.

I know that what I'm about to share is an inconvenient truth. As I travel, I can see that there is an unsettledness in the hearts of men and women who serve in church leadership. They are tired of looking at the same faces and feeding an already bloated carcass when there's a world out there to conquer. To these passionate believers, church within the four walls has become unbearable— and I can't blame them!

THEY ARE AS MUCH A STRANGER TO THE GOSPEL AS THE ATHEIST AND AS MUCH AN ALIEN TO THE PROMISES OF GOD AS AN AGNOSTIC.

I know that many of us are just plain done with church as usual and are ready to break out in search of something more. But before we go, we have to ask ourselves a question: "If we can't stand to be within the four walls, why on earth do we want to go out there and invite hurting people into them?" When surrounded by this kind of decadence, debauchery, and igno-

---

7 Ed Stetzer, "Barna: How Many Have a Biblical Worldview?" *CT*, March 09, 2009, accessed February 02, 2019, http://www.christianitytoday.com/edstetzer/2009/march.

rance within our own ranks, evangelism as we have known it must become suspect. How can we attempt to obey the Great Commission when it seems like there's a Great Conspiracy in the church itself? If this sounds strange, it's language that God Himself used in describing the conditions in Judah during Jeremiah's day:

> *And the LORD said unto me, A conspiracy is found among the men of Judah, and among the inhabitants of Jerusalem. They are turned back to the iniquities of their forefathers, which refused to hear my words; and they went after other gods to serve them: the house of Israel and the house of Judah have broken my covenant which I made with their fathers (Jeremiah 11:9–10).*

At that time the conspiracy was to forsake the true and living God and return to following idols. The conspiracy now doesn't seem to be all that different. The idols just have different names.

I submit to you that all we are managing to do right now with our evangelism is scratch an itch. I know that we think fresh blood will bring excitement to the crowd, but a handful of new converts can't change a twenty-year old culture of dead traditionalism or lazy Pentecostalism. On the contrary! The *new* will eventually be swallowed up into the same *old* system we've come to detest.

"Are you saying we shouldn't evangelize?" No! I am saying that in order to truly be effective, we have to find our footing and do things God's way. What do we do in times like these when the physician is both ailing and contagious? Should we send the sick doctor out to infect more with his illness, or should we treat the doctor first so that he can effectively administer the cure to others?

> *For I am not ashamed of the gospel of Christ: for it is the power of God unto salvation to everyone that believeth; to the Jew first, and also to the Greek. For therein is the righteousness of God revealed from faith to faith: as it is written, the just shall live by faith (Romans 1:16–17).*

This is a very familiar passage of Scripture, yet there is a portion of it that often gets overlooked which says, "To the Jew first." Here we see a principle: there is a divine prerogative of priority outlined to the Jew *first*. I'm not sure how we missed it, but it has been there all along. We see it in the ministry of Jesus when He declares in Matthew 15:24 that He has come *only* to the lost sheep of the house of Israel, then again in His command in Acts 1:8 that we are to be His witnesses in Jerusalem, Judea, Samaria and the uttermost parts of the earth. Consistently we see this same precedent, even in the commission of the great apostle Paul himself who preached *first* to the Jews.

What is the principle? God's priority rests first with *His* people—and then with the rest of the world. God focuses on His children first, and then He focuses on expansion by adoption. It should be noted here that I am merely pointing out a principle. I do not believe that the church or anyone else has replaced the Jewish people. There is much to be said about making the Jewish people and the nation of Israel a priority—which we do at Encounter Christ Church where I pastor. However, here I am simply pointing out the order and values expressed by God throughout His Word.

1 Timothy suggests very strongly that our initial focus should be on providing for our own family:

> *If any provide not for his own, and specially for those of his own house, he hath denied the faith, and is worse than an infidel (1 Timothy 5:8).*

> *When Paul says, "therein is the righteousness of God revealed from faith to faith" (Romans 1:17), he is telling us that we must first start with the faith we're in before we try to reach the next faith with the gospel. If our evangelism has felt forced and is not as effective as we know it should be, it is because we have been operating half-blind. Before we can go out there and remove the splinter from the world's eye, we need to first remove the mote from our own eye (Matthew 7:3–5).*

Before we can be effective witnesses for the kingdom, we must "tarry… in the city of Jerusalem until [we] be endued with power from on high" (Luke 24:49). It's time to clean house! If we truly want to reach the world, we must first get our own houses in order.

> *For the time is come that judgment must begin at the house of God: and if it first begin at us, what shall the end be of them that obey not the gospel of God? And if the righteous scarcely be saved, where shall the ungodly and the sinner appear?… Elders…you I exhort…: Feed the flock which is among you, taking the oversight thereof (1 Peter 4:17–18; 5:1–2).*

In Luke 15, Jesus shares a parable about a woman who lost a coin. He tells us that when she realized something was missing, she did not go and invite her friends and neighbors over. It was only after she got her house in order and found what was missing that she went out to her neighbors.

Until we have disciples and not just church attendees, until we have converts and not just informal followers, we will never be able to reach the world beyond our church walls. How can we ask people to help others become committed to the cause of Christ when we are not truly committed themselves?

In an age where the house of God is in such disarray, we must look at evangelism differently. I am not saying that we shouldn't witness. We can—and should—but we can't leave the other undone. The church is currently operating like a restaurant which, after failing its heath inspection, has determined to invest all its money in advertising.

I have stated already that our western culture has undoubtedly defined church success for us, and it can be summed up in two words: *attendance* and *acceptance*. We've been sold a bill of goods, and we have fallen for it hook, line, and sinker.

The body of Christ is desperately trying to be accepted, so it attempts to increase attendance by waging massive PR campaigns, designed to win hearts and minds through carefully organized outreaches and charity events. These things in and of themselves can be wonderful, but they can also be self-defeating.

I would like to tell you a parable about a man who had five children. These children were well cared for by their father. Over time, several of his children became spoiled—particularly his toddlers. The father decided to remove some of their comforts and take them out into the world to share what they had with the needy.

Reluctant at first, the children eventually warmed up to the idea, and the father began to see the change he was looking for in their hearts. He became the talk of the town. Not only were his children blessed, but their good works were lauded in the city. This encouraged the father to give even more and to work tirelessly to help the less fortunate. Days turned into weeks, and weeks turned into months, as this father gave all that he had to the poor and hungry. He left his job and worked sunup to sundown with the local orphanage. He would leave before his children awoke in the morning and not get home until after they went to bed. They wanted to spend more time with their daddy, but they knew that what he was doing was just and good.

Knowing that his children were healthy and could miss a few meals, he would often take the food they would have eaten that day and give it to the homeless. His children, wanting to help and unable to argue with the immense needs of these hurting people, didn't complain. After some time, his own children became malnourished and sick. His children were starving—while he gave food to the world's children.

Consumed with the urgency of his own mission, the father argued that they should be able to provide for themselves, and so they did...or at least they tried. After the youngest died, the others tried to make sense of it all and provide for themselves without the guidance of their father. Three of the middle children left home never to return, but the oldest stuck with his dad until he had a family of his own.

God's children are starving while we give the devil's kids thousands of pounds of groceries. Some may allege that we are all God's children, but that's a lie. If we were all God's children we wouldn't need to be born again. We should not neglect the poor and the needy of this world based on their religious affiliation or lack thereof, but the divine prerogative stands: God's house and God's people are first. We have churches giving out thousands of dollars in gas cards to random people while members of their own congregations are struggling to make it to church on Sunday. This ought not be!

GOD'S HOUSE AND GOD'S PEOPLE ARE FIRST.

Here's a question to meditate on: What would happen if we took care of our own first?

We've been giving the milk out for free and wondering why they're not buying the cow. Let's take care of our own, and the world will be lining up to get into the church! Gideon, after all, had to have his own encounter before he could seek to lead others into theirs. How can we take someone where we've never been? How can we show them something we've never seen? Gideon says, "Before I take on the world, I need to encounter Christ for myself!"

This will require a lot of grace and an abundance of humility. This will demand a fresh look at our church practices and a clear understanding of our church priorities. This will necessitate a new definition of our *mission*, and of our *new mission field*.

CHAPTER 8: QUESTIONS FOR REFLECTION

1. George Barna uncovered some revealing statistics about modern Christians. How would you answer the following questions?

   • Do you believe Satan is real?

   • Do you believe there is such a thing as absolute truth?

   • Do you believe abortion should be legal?

   • Do you believe marriage should be redefined?

   • What is a biblical worldview?

2. What examples can you think of that illustrate how the modern church needs to be re-evangelized?

3. What are some ways that we can improve the church to make it ready for new converts?

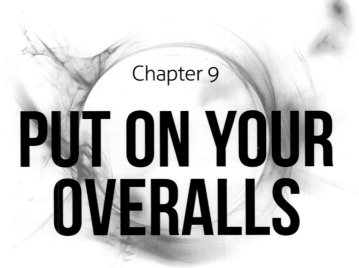

Chapter 9

PUT ON YOUR OVERALLS

"Be humble or you'll stumble."
—Dwight L. Moody[1]

"A man's pride shall bring him low: but honour shall uphold the humble in spirit" (Proverbs 29:23).

Oh, how entitled the average believer has become! We trample over the sacred and secularize the holy through our misapplied right to, "come boldly unto the throne of grace" (Hebrews 4:16). This small anecdote described this condition well:

"On a visit to the Beethoven museum in Bonn, a young American student became fascinated by the piano on which Beethoven had composed some of

---

1 Dwight L. Moody, "Dwight L. Moody Quote," *A-Z Quotes,* accessed February 02, 2019, https://www.azquotes.com/quote/757557.

his greatest works. She asked the museum guard if she could play a few bars on it; she accompanied the request with a lavish tip, and the guard agreed. The girl went to the piano and tinkled out the opening of the Moonlight Sonata. As she was leaving she said to the guard, 'I suppose all the great pianists who come here want to play on that piano.' The guard shook his head. 'Padarewski [the famed Polish pianist] was here a few years ago and he said he wasn't worthy to touch it.'"[2]

LEARNING TO PRAY SUCCESSFULLY ISN'T ALWAYS AS IMPORTANT AS LEARNING TO REMOVE THOSE HINDRANCES THAT BLOCK SUCCESSFUL PRAYING.

Humility is a necessary ingredient for every Christian. It's important for every believer to know how to pray effectively; but before we step into the arena of prayer, it's important that we have the right attire for the occasion. The Bible says to "be clothed with humility: for God resisteth the proud, and giveth grace to the humble" (1 Peter 5:5). Learning to pray successfully isn't always as important as learning to remove those hindrances that block successful praying.

The first step in removing hindrances to our prayer life is to clothe ourselves with humility. One translation tells us to put on the "overall" of humility:

You younger members must also submit to the elders. Indeed all of you should defer to one another and wear the "overall" of humility in serving each other. 'God resists the proud, but gives grace to the humble' (1 Peter 5:5, PHILLIPS).

In the same way that clothes protect us from the elements and exposure, humility will protect us from the storms of life.

Inevitably, some religious temple guards (the keepers of how things "ought to be") will exclaim, "Oh, don't you dare pray for patience! God will humble you!" Are these spiritual wet blankets correct? Are there things we should be afraid to pray for? I don't think I could answer this question with a more emphatic, "No!"

Don't be afraid to pray for humility—or anything else for that matter. God is not going to hurt you— *ever.* "Well Pastor, I read in the Bible where God cursed so and so" What many people are unaware of is that there is a difference between the permissive verb tense and the causative verb tense. When we read in the Old Testament that "God smote them," these statements are in the permissive verb tense and can literally be translated, "God had to allow them to be smitten" *because of their disobedience.* Let's look at what 1 Peter 5 says:

> *Be clothed with humility: for God resisteth the proud, and giveth grace to the humble. Humble yourselves therefore under the mighty hand of God, that he may exalt you in due time (1 Peter 5:5–6).*

I'M PROUD OF MY HUMILITY!

If humility is one of our greatest assets in prayer, pride is our greatest liability. God resists and refuses to go along with the proud. What is pride? What is humility?

Contrary to popular opinion, humility is not self-debasement, and pride is much more than a haughty attitude. Let's add one more verse to the context of 1 Peter so that we can get a better understanding of what this apostle is trying to tell us:

> *Be clothed with humility: for God resisteth the proud, and giveth grace to the humble. Humble yourselves therefore under the mighty hand of God...casting all your care upon him; for He careth for you (1 Peter 5:5–7).*

Here is the focal point: Real humility is "casting all your care upon Him." So, what is this evil thing called pride? What is it about pride that is so repugnant that God resists it and refuses to go along with it (Proverbs 16:18)? *Pride is caring for our own cares.* We'd like to think of pride as something scandalous, outrageous, and uncommon—at least in our own lives. Regrettably, it's far less offensive to our senses than we'd like to think, and it's so common that we've become very comfortable with it.

Pride is so insidious that it most often disguises itself—with the aid of religious tradition—as humility and can lie unnoticed for years as it wraps its tentacles around the heart of the Christian.

How can we tell if we've been infected? The symptoms are easy to spot if we know what we're looking for. If we hear the following statements come out of our own mouths, we may be dealing with a major infestation of pride:

"*I* don't know how *I'm* going to get through this."

"*I* can't take this anymore."

"God, *I'm* just so unworthy."

And the *coup de grâce*: "*I'm* just an old sinner!"

It may be religiously correct to make such statements, but they are actually pride masquerading as humility. When we say that *we* don't know how *we're* going to get through this, or *we* can't take this anymore, we're saying that *we* have taken the responsibility of caring for our own cares. When we say *we* are unworthy or "just an old sinner saved by grace," *we* are taking the burden of our sin and our worth on our own shoulders. This is pride at its best.

WE'RE NOT SINNERS SAVED BY GRACE

If we take the time to think about it, we'll realize that this really is a masterful deception, and that's why it has ensnared millions of Christians. Are we just old sinners, or have we been saved (transformed into a new creature) by grace? We can't be both!

The prideful *take on the care* of their past sins. The humble, on the other hand, *cast the care* of their past onto the Lord. They allow their sins to be thrown into the sea of forgetfulness, all the while accepting a new life, with a new identity and a clean rap sheet.

Here's 1 Peter 5:7 in the Amplified Bible:

Casting all your cares [all your anxieties, all your worries, and all your concerns, once and for all] on Him, for He cares about you [with deepest affection, and watches over you very carefully (1 Peter 5:7, AMP).

Humility is truly a virtue that destroys all the hyphenated self-sins of our day, from self-indulgence to self-sufficiency. Humility paves the way for success in prayer because it unlocks the greatest power in the universe. If God can find those who will humble themselves (notice that He will not do it *for* them—or *to* them), then He will give them something called *grace*. Humility releases the divine force of grace into our lives.

> **HUMILITY PAVES THE WAY FOR SUCCESS IN PRAYER BECAUSE IT UNLOCKS THE GREATEST POWER IN THE UNIVERSE.**

Like many things of importance in God's Word, the traditions of the church have attempted to rob any real power or meaning out of the word *grace* to the point that we really don't know what it is any more. We think that maybe grace is just a distant cousin to mercy—or perhaps it's just a likable personality trait that God has, which allows Him to put up with us.

Grace is so much more than anything we have learned or imagined. Here are some verses we can meditate on that will help us come to a greater understanding of the meaning of the grace that God has promised to give to those who "cast their care" on Him:

> *But God, who is rich in mercy, for his great love wherewith he loved us, Even when we were dead in sins, hath quickened us together with Christ, (by grace ye are saved;) and hath raised us up together, and made us sit together in heavenly places in Christ Jesus: that in the ages to come he might shew the exceeding riches of his grace in his kindness toward us through Christ Jesus. For by grace are ye saved through faith (Ephesians 2:4–8).*

> *Not by works of righteousness which we have done, but according to his mercy he saved us, by the washing of regeneration, and renewing of the Holy Ghost; which he shed on us abundantly through Jesus Christ our Saviour; that being justified by his grace, we should be made heirs according to the hope of eternal life (Titus 3:5–7).*

What is it that is powerful enough to save the vilest sinner? Grace! How can someone be born again, and be totally transformed and translated from darkness to light? Grace! In fact, Paul says that we have been "quickened (made alive) together with Christ" (Ephesians 2:5, addition mine) by the power of grace. Grace is even powerful enough to *justify* us.

To be *justified* means to have our past wiped away to the point that it is "just-as-if-I'd" never sinned. The awesome power of grace has the ability to remove our past from the sight of the all-seeing, infinite One Himself. Praise God, now that's some amazing grace! I like what Philippians 4 says in *The Message*:

Don't fret or worry. Instead of worrying, pray. Let petitions and praises shape your worries into prayers...Before you know it, a sense of God's wholeness, everything coming together for good, will come and settle you down. It's wonderful what happens when Christ displaces worry at the center of your life (Philippians 4:6, MSG).

All we must do to receive this wonder-working power into our lives is humble ourselves under the mighty hand of God and cast all our care on Him.

> Let's not wait another minute; let's do that right now! We can take our care, our anxiety, and our need for control: recognize it as pride, and cast it onto the shoulders of the One who's able and willing to bear it. We just might find ourselves rejoicing with the apostle Paul in saying, "Your grace is sufficient for me" (2 Corinthians 12:9).

Gideon's cry should be one of real humility with a confidence that rests solely in the One who redeemed us. Pride can rear its ugly head as a disrespectful sense of entitlement and unfounded self-assurance; or disguised as humility, it can show itself wearing a garment of self-righteousness and unworthiness. As unusual as this may sound, these two deceptions can exist in the same mind, producing an ungodly inner conflict that will tear the soul apart.

THE DEATH OF A DOUBLE MIND

What does it mean to be double-minded? A mother noticed that a friend of her teenage daughter had a tattoo of a Japanese symbol on her back.

"Please don't tell my parents," the girl begged.

"I won't," the mother promised. "By the way, what does that stand for?"

"Honesty," the girl replied.[3]

That is double-mindedness!

Why do prayers go unanswered? Why does victory seem lost? Why is shallow spirituality becoming the norm in the American church? Double-mindedness! James focuses on this very point:

> *Let not that man think that he shall receive any thing of the Lord. A double-minded man is unstable in all his ways (James 1:7–8).*

Wouldn't it have been amazing to be a fly on the wall in Jesus' home? What insights could we have gleaned from years of living in the same house with Jesus? The author of these words had just that advantage! James was the younger brother of our Lord and had lived with Him his entire life. This fact may explain his pithy candor as he in no uncertain terms says, "Let not a double-minded man think that he shall receive anything from *my brother*" (James 1:7–8, the italicized section is my paraphrase).

Religion makes prayer as clear as mud, but James expressed this truth as though it were as plain as the nose on our face: Double-mindedness robs Christians of their victory in Christ and causes them to fall prey to the Enemy of their souls. The battle for the success of our Christian life is fought in the arena of our mind. This is where the Enemy utilizes all his resources.

---

3 Byron Martin, "Tempted And Double-Minded," *Sermon Central*, January 12, 2010, accessed February 03, 2019, https://www.sermoncentral.com/sermons/tempted-and-double-minded-byron-martin-sermon-on-doubt-142974?ref=SermonSerps.

He's not after our jobs—he doesn't need them! He's not after our house or our family either. His primary goal is to bombard our minds by causing havoc in these areas of our lives.

Beloved, I wish above all things that thou mayest prosper and be in health, even as thy soul prospereth (3 John 2:2).

The prosperity of our outward life is directly connected to the prosperity of our inward life! The Devil knows that if he can make us mentally sick, then he can make us physically sick. Do we have a mind to be blessed? Perhaps a better question is: Do we have a mind to change? The Bible says, "As he (a man) thinketh in his heart, so is he" (Proverbs 23:7, addition mine).

THE PROSPERITY OF OUR OUTWARD LIFE IS DIRECTLY CONNECTED TO THE PROSPERITY OF OUR INWARD LIFE!

The blessing of God cannot be received or sustained by an unrenewed mind.

I beseech you therefore, brethren, by the mercies of God, that ye present your bodies a living sacrifice, holy, acceptable unto God, which is your reasonable service. And be not conformed to this world: but be ye transformed by the renewing of your mind (Romans 12:1–2).

We've got to dump out all pettiness, all bitterness, all unforgiveness, and every inflexibility. We've got to renew our minds because it is with our minds that we serve the Lord!

Do you recall the location where our Prince, Savior, and Older Brother was crucified? It was called *Golgotha,* which can be interpreted as "the place of the skull." The territory of the unrenewed mind is the beachhead of satanic assault in our lives.

Satan is the original zombie. The judgment of God in Genesis 3 upon him was that he would "eat dust" (Genesis 3:14), and in case we've forgotten, we've got that in common: "For dust thou art!" (Genesis 3:19). That's our carnal nature. Satan feeds off our carnality!

> *To be carnally minded is death; but to be spiritually minded is life and peace. Because the carnal mind is enmity against God: for it is not subject to the law of God, neither indeed can be. So then they that are in the flesh cannot please God (Romans 8:6–8).*

Double-mindedness is standing in two boats at the same time—with one foot in each. A double-minded person dances around the truth while thinking they're embracing it. A double-minded person prays, but doubts (James 1:5–8). A double-minded person is constantly on an emotional rollercoaster—up one day and down the next. A double-minded person hears the Word but does not act upon it (James 1:22–25). James says that if any of this describes us, then we should know that we won't receive anything from the Lord. It's no wonder our nation is in its current condition: The church is as double-minded as can be!

Double-mindedness isn't merely confusion either. Double-mindedness is the eating away of the redeemed mindset. A person with this split in their soul will believe in healing with all their heart and yet deep down feel unworthy to receive it. A double-minded person will believe it's God's will to bless them, while at the same time feeling undeserving to walk in His blessing. A double-minded person knows that God loves them yet feels fearful and insecure all the time. Double-mindedness and a revelation of the grace of God cannot coexist in the same heart. Have we allowed condemnation to take hold of our souls and undermine our faith? It's time to rise up and, with a Gideon's cry, take hold of our confidence in Christ once again!

What can we do if we find ourselves with a double mind? According to James 4:8, we must draw near to God, change our ways, change our heart, and resist the Devil! Dive into God's Word: Hear it, read it, speak it, and obey it! God's Word and faith in His Word is the only remedy for a double mind.

CHAPTER 9: QUESTIONS FOR REFLECTION

1. Real humility is "casting all your cares upon Him." Describe an occasion when you cast all your cares on God.

2. Pride sometimes disguises itself as humility. Have you seen evidence of this in your life, or in the life of someone you know? How might this stop the power of God from working in that situation?

3. Pride is "caring for our own cares." Has there ever been a time when you were tempted to take care of an issue or problem yourself, rather than asking for God's help? What was the outcome? How do you think it might have been different if you had given the care of it to God first?

4. Have you ever displayed the characteristics of double-mindedness? Have you ever allowed condemnation to push you away from the reviving presence of God? What can you do to fight this?

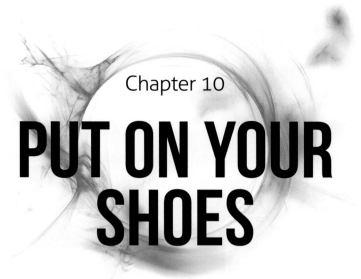

Chapter 10

PUT ON YOUR SHOES

"Can't you stick it out with me a single hour?" (Matthew 26:40, MSG).

"And Joshua said unto the people, Sanctify yourselves: for to morrow the LORD *will do wonders among you"* (Joshua 3:5).

If the First Great Awakening was a revival of preaching and repentance, the Second Great Awakening was a revival of preaching and prayer.

To many, what God was doing in the Second Great Awakening took precedence over everything else in their lives. Finney himself missed his own honeymoon. Finney was married on October 5, 1824. He went to bring her possessions from Evans Mills, and he was expected to be back in a week. Every town and village he went through, however, begged him to stay. Six months later, instead of returning home, he had to send for his wife to come be with him instead. Revival services would go on for more than twenty days, with prayer meetings at one time of day, a meeting for those wanting salvation at another time of day, and then general services in the evening. Nearly all the adult population of a city of thousands would be converted.

Finney urged the people to pray to God earnestly and expectantly for the immediate outpouring of the Holy Spirit. He told them that if they united in prayer, they would get God's answer "quicker than a letter could come from Albany, the state's capital."[1] The same is true for us today! If we unite in prayer, things will happen quickly.

In every town where this revival took hold, the voices of prayer could be heard continually. Go wherever you wanted in the town, and you would find people praying. Walk along the streets, and if Christians happened to run into each other, they ended up praying.

One merchant arrived by stagecoach to do business in a city where Finney had been, but found that it "was all religion." Wherever he tried to do business, people witnessed to him. The merchant became so disgusted that he decided to leave by stagecoach right away, but when the hotel manager heard his remarks he took him aside and prayed with him. Before he could get on the stagecoach, he was gloriously saved. Now, instead of continuing on his business trip, he went home and began to witness. He won his family to the Lord and began to boldly witness until a great revival came to his town through his testimony.[2] This is just one example of the thousands that were bathed in the atmosphere of real prayer.

---

1   Wesley L. Duewel, *Revival Fire* (Grand Rapids, MI: Zondervan, 1995), 101.

2   Ibid. 102.

In Christian circles, we often speak in lofty platitudes that may spark a passion for change in the lives of believers, but we rarely deliver the type of practical knowledge that will provide the kindling to keep the fires of change burning. Gideon's cry brought about change in his circumstances. It's important for us to note that the Bible warns us of trumpets that give an uncertain sound. It is not enough to just *cry*; it has to be the *right* cry. I like to say it this way: It's not enough to *pray*, we've got to pray *right*.

IT'S NOT ENOUGH TO PRAY, WE'VE GOT TO PRAY RIGHT.

We know that repentance gives us access into the presence of God, but access doesn't guarantee an audience. We might be granted access to the White House, but if we walk in there with the wrong attitude and attire we'll be escorted out quickly.

For the Gideons who are asking, "Where is the power?" our prayer lives would be a good place to start the search. After working in an international prayer center for many years and fielding prayer requests from all over the world, I have discovered that scores of people are just plain oblivious when it comes to prayer!

I'm not exaggerating; in fact, I am *understating* the problem. I can clearly remember one of my first days on the job. I was so excited to have the honor of standing in faith with people who were believing for God to work miracles in their lives. My innocent delusions of agreement in prayer soon came crashing down with one of my first calls. The call was from a woman who wanted me to pray for God to kill her son's pediatrician! "Oh, don't worry," she said," He deserves it!" Apparently, he had suggested that her nine-year-old son ought to be able to tie his own shoes by now.

This may sound extreme, but the truth is that if something is blocking our fellowship with God or hindering our prayers from being answered, there's no difference in results between the person who prays for God to kill someone and the one who prays concerning the healing of a deadly disease with, "Lord, if it be Thy will…" Of course, the emotional and mental state of the individual praying for outright murder is beyond insane and cannot be compared to someone's naïve prayers, yet both are praying in ignorance, *and neither will be answered.*

From vain repetitions to pinheaded petitions, the prayer warrior, in today's church, has become a crapshooter! We don't really know if it's going to work, but, "Come on, Jesus! Daddy needs a new pair of shoes!"

Thankfully, it doesn't have to be this way. There are some simple things anyone can do that will transform him or her into a person whose prayers are answered every time! Too often the profundity of prayer keeps us from realizing its simultaneous simplicity. Prayer is not solely for the super-saint or the hyper-spiritual. A successful prayer life is, at this moment, within our reach! For most of us, our struggle is that we have never had genuine prayer modeled before us.

THE KEY IS PREPARATION

There is a veritable treasure trove of truth hiding in Paul's teaching on the armor of God, waiting to be uncovered as we study God's Word:

> *For we wrestle not against flesh and blood, but against principalities, against powers, against the rulers of the darkness of this world, against spiritual wickedness in high places. Wherefore take unto you the whole armour of God, that ye may be able to withstand in the evil day, and having done all, to stand...your feet shod with the preparation of the gospel of peace (Ephesians 6:12–13,15).*

Paul reveals that we are under constant attack and that this Christian *walk* is more of a *sprint*—directly into enemy-held territory! That being said, no battle can be successfully waged off the cuff when we have time, or if we get around to it. God has given us some very helpful weaponry and armor to assist us in this war.

Of all the attire Paul lists in Ephesians 6, there is one item that I want to focus on: our shoes. Famed comedian Steven Wright once said: "I was sad because I had no shoes, until I met a man who had no feet. So I said, 'Got any shoes you're not using?'"[3] If Christians don't learn to "shod" their feet properly, the Enemy will steal those feet right out from under them.

Paul admonished us to have our feet "shod with the preparation of the gospel of peace" (Ephesians 6:15). In our normal, everyday lives, where does peace come from? If we were required to take a test on thermodynamics or quantitative molecular biological engineering today and the results would determine the next five years of our lives, would we have peace? Probably not! Why? Because we're not prepared to answer the questions on

---

3 Steven Wright, "A Quote by Steven Wright," *Goodreads*, accessed February 04, 2019, https://www.goodreads.com/quotes/96928-i-was-sad-because-i-had-no-shoes.

that type of test!

Preparation produces the kind of peace that Paul is talking about. Believe it or not, there are people in the world who have studied quantitative molecular biological engineering and are adequately prepared to be tested on it. I'm not one of them, but I have learned how to prepare for prayer!

Paul is saying that if we want to have sure footing, we need to be prepared. Our preparation will remove the anxiety of the unknown. Like any good soldier knows, the training they receive prepares them to be able to function in battle. If we will take these simple steps, we can go from praying to praying *right*. We will begin to see changes not only in how we pray, but also in our relationship with God.

LET OUR PRAYER TIME BE HOLY

Too often, Christians randomly select an available time during their day and simply pray about whatever crosses their minds. After a few minutes of this tedious exercise, they run out of things to say, their mind gets distracted by impending daily responsibilities, they lose focus, and begin to wonder, *How in the world can anyone pray for thirty minutes, much less for an hour?* Does any of that sound familiar? Sure, it does! We've all struggled with that type of thinking, but, thank God, it doesn't have to be that way. If we adequately prepare for our time with God, the only difficulty we'll have is wondering where the time went!

Prayer comes in many forms, shapes, and sizes. As Christians, prayer should not be just a daily or even an hourly activity; it should be continuous. First Thessalonians 5:17 instructs us to "pray without ceasing." Prayer centers on our relationship with God. We can easily communicate with God while driving down the road or sitting at our desk in the office. If the only time we ever spoke with our spouse was during times like these, we wouldn't have much of a relationship with them, would we?

In order for a marriage to work, we need set aside time just for our spouse. I've seen marriages fall apart because parents were so busy with their careers and their children that they rarely took time to talk to each other. Then, once the children left the nest, they didn't know how to communicate with one another.

If the only time we communicate with our heavenly Father is in the middle of our busy day, we'll fail to find the power that awaits us in a real relationship with Him. We need to set aside a time just for God in our day-to-day lives: a *holy* time.

WE NEED TO SET ASIDE A TIME JUST FOR GOD IN OUR DAY-TO-DAY LIVES: A HOLY TIME.

What does the Bible mean when it says that God is *holy*? The word *holy* has many connotations. It means to be pure, consecrated, and separated. God is *holy* because He is absolutely separate from the world. If we desire a *holy* God to commune with us, it will benefit us to have a *holy* time for Him to meet with us. Consider it as being a sort of "divine bait" that God can't resist.

I encourage you to schedule a time each day that is separated just for you and God and allow nothing to interrupt that time. The disciples had a regular time of prayer: Acts 3:1 tells us that, "Peter and John went up together into the temple at the hour of prayer." That was a set time!

We see another set time of prayer when Pharaoh begged Moses to pray that God would take away the plague of frogs from Egypt:

> *"You set the time!" Moses replied. "Tell me when you want me*
> *to pray for you, your officials, and your people. Then you and*
> *your houses will be rid of the frogs" (Exodus 8:9, NLT).*

If we want to be free, we need to set a time to pray! There are, of course, those casual seekers who will say that this is not a possibility in today's world in which people have families, careers, and a multitude of daily activities that prevent this type of prayer. I made the same argument until the Holy Spirit showed me that, right in the middle of the busiest seasons in my life, I somehow found time to make appointments with the doctor, the dentist, and the car mechanic!

Author Jean McMahon recalls this incident: "Attending church in Kentucky, we watched an especially verbal and boisterous child being hurried out, slung under his irate father's arm. No one in the congregation so much as raised an eyebrow—until the child captured everyone's attention by crying out in a charming Southern accent, 'Ya'll pray for me now!'"[4]

That child was ready to make time for prayer! Are we ready to make time for prayer? When we perceive something as important, we will make time for it—no matter how inconvenient it may be. Friends, prayer is important!

---

4 "Naughty Child," *Bible.org*, accessed February 04, 2019, https://bible.org/illustration/naughty-child.

In fact, I believe it is the most important thing we can do in a day:

"Early African converts to Christianity were earnest and regular in private devotions. Each one reportedly had a separate spot in the thicket where he would pour out his heart to God. Over time the paths to these places became well worn. As a result, if one of these believers began to neglect prayer, it was soon apparent to the others. They would kindly remind the negligent one, 'Brother, the grass grows on your path.'"[5]

Is the grass growing on your path? When we make that appointment with God and keep it daily, He'll show up before we do, and it will radically increase the effectiveness of our time with Him. Whether it is after everyone in our home is asleep at night, or before anyone is up in the morning, set the time and make it holy.

---

5 "The Grass Grows on Your Path," *Ministry127*, accessed February 04, 2019, http://ministry127. com/resources/illustration/the-grass-grows-on-your-path.

CHAPTER 10: QUESTIONS FOR REFLECTION

1. How would it make you feel if someone offered to pray with you while you were in a public place, with others nearby who could hear him praying? What does that say about our personal prayer lives?

2. Discuss the concept: "preparation produces peace." Have you ever spent time in prayer preparing for an important event in your life? How did this affect the situation?

3. Do you have a certain time each day set apart for prayer? If not, how can you change that today?

4. "Does the grass grow on your path?" What does that question mean to you?

Chapter 11

LEAVE YOUR DRAMA AT THE DOOR

"Drama is very important in life…Everything can have drama if it's done right. Even a pancake." —Julia Child[1]

"And when thou prayest, thou shalt not be as the hypocrites are: for they love to pray standing in the synagogues and in the corners of the streets, that they may be seen of men. Verily I say unto you, they have their reward" (Matthew 6:5).

Like the little boy in the previous chapter who was about to have the rod of correction applied to the seat of his understanding, many of us have a flair for the dramatic—and that's putting it lightly. Within the western church, we have more drama than a reality show! Whether it's something as grave

---

1 Julia Child, "Julia Child Quotes," *BrainyQuote*, accessed February 05, 2019, https://www. brainyquote.com/quotes/julia_child_442470

as divorce or as benign as a headache, we tend to seek sympathy—whether it be from God or our own colleagues. The problem with attempting to gain God's attention with the severity of our need is that it doesn't work. In fact, I would go so far as to say that this hinders God's ability to bring us into the fullness of His desire for our lives.

If we want to have a great time with God in prayer and give birth to a new awakening in our lives, we must be disciplined enough to leave all our drama at the door. This may sound harsh to a few, because the only reason many ever go to God is for help with some temporal, emotional need. There are some who only see prayer as a spare tire instead of a place of relationship and communication.

Am I saying we shouldn't share these types of emotional needs with God, or that we can't be honest with Him about how we truly feel? Certainly not! God cares about all of our struggles—large and small. But how many friends would we have if we began every conversation with them by unloading our problems and asking them for help? The place of prayer is more than a one-stop, quick fix for all our problems. The place of prayer is a place of relationship and communion.

Think about the kind of people you enjoy being around. Are they always depressed? Are they always talking about their needs? Do they always say the same thing over and over and over? Yet, this is what most of our prayers are like!

On the other hand, we all like hanging around people who always seem to have an encouraging spirit about them! Isn't it great to fellowship with people who have a hopeful demeanor no matter what they're facing in life?

There are some people who make us feel better just by being around them. In fact, if we find someone like that, we'll go out of our way to be around them. Like us, God wants to be around people with the right spirit.

> *But the hour cometh, and now is, when the true worshippers shall worship the Father in spirit and in truth: for the Father seeketh such to worship him. God is a Spirit: and they that worship him must worship him in spirit and in truth (John 4:23–24).*

From these verses, it's obvious that God is looking for a certain kind of person to hang out with.

In the story of the Syrophoenician woman, we see a woman with tremendous problems and a lot of drama at home. Her own daughter is being tormented by demonic spirits! It is difficult to see someone we love being ravaged by addiction, disease, or tragedy. Our hearts break when it seems like there is nothing we can do to help them, especially if it is our own child.

> *Then Jesus went thence, and departed into the coasts of Tyre and Sidon. And, behold, a woman of Canaan came out of the same coasts, and cried unto him, saying, Have mercy on me, O Lord, thou son of David; my daughter is grievously vexed with a devil (Matthew 15:21–22).*

Here was a mother who thought her daughter was going to die. I don't imagine she spoke quietly as she called out for help from Jesus. In fact, the disciples were so disturbed by the commotion she was making that they wanted to send her away. Jesus' response was not what the disciples—or the woman—expected.

But he answered her not a word. And his disciples came and besought him, saying, Send her away; for she crieth after us. But he answered and said, I am not sent but unto the lost sheep of the house of Israel (Matthew 15:23–24).

The woman realized it was going to take a different approach to connect with Jesus—and she found that way in worship.

Then came she and worshipped him, saying, Lord, help me. But he answered and said, It is not meet to take the children's bread, and to cast it to dogs. And she said, Truth, Lord: yet the dogs eat of the crumbs which fall from their masters' table. Then Jesus answered and said unto her, O woman, great is thy faith: be it unto thee even as thou wilt. And her daughter was made whole from that very hour (Matthew 15:25–28).

GOD CANNOT RESPOND SIMPLY BECAUSE WE HAVE A NEED, NO MATTER HOW AUTHENTIC THAT NEED MAY BE.

This woman may have been warranted in her frantic attempt to find help for her daughter, but the key she discovered was the faith that was released through her worship. We may be justified in our feelings of desperation when we come to God in prayer, but we must learn that God cannot respond simply because we have a need, no matter how authentic that need may be. God can only respond to those who approach Him with a heart of faith. The proof of this is found in verse 23: "He answered her not a word."

This is startling! Here we have a woman God loves, crying out to Him for help—yet, "he answered her not a word." Have you ever cried out to God but heard no answer? At one time or another, we all have. What we need to realize is that silence from heaven is not normal, and it's not acceptable!

I read once that a small town in America had been historically "dry" (without alcohol) when a local businessman decided to build a tavern. A group of Christians from a local church were concerned and planned an all-night prayer meeting to ask God to intervene. It just so happened that shortly after their prayer meeting, lightning struck the bar, and it burned to the ground. The owner of the bar sued the church, claiming that the prayers of the church were responsible, but the church hired a lawyer to argue in court that they were not responsible. The presiding judge, after his initial review of the case, stated, "No matter how this case comes out, one thing is clear. The tavern owner believes in prayer, and the Christians do not!"[2]

My dear friend, I want you to know that prayer works, and God wants to answer our prayers. The Bible declares in Jeremiah 33:3, "Call unto me, and I will answer thee."

The God of the Bible is a prayer-answering God. Moses prayed and quenched the fire of God's wrath against Israel. Joshua prayed and made the very rotation of the earth stop. Hannah prayed, and God gave her a son named Samuel. Elijah prayed, and God sent fire from heaven to consume the sacrifice. Nehemiah prayed, and God allowed him to rebuild the bro-

---

2 "Prayer Devotionals and Illustrations," *Precept Austin*, accessed February 06, 2019, https://www.preceptaustin.org/prayer_devotionals_and_illustrations.

ken-down walls of the city of Jerusalem. The Bible says that God "turned the captivity of Job" (Job 42:10) and gave him double when he prayed for his friends. Daniel prayed, and God shut the mouths of lions. Jesus prayed, the disciples prayed, and you I can call out to the same God with full assurance of faith that the answer is on the way.

We have somehow managed to lull ourselves into a false sense of comfort regarding unanswered prayer. We have become accustomed to Him answering "not a word," when the Bible clearly says, "If ye shall ask any thing in my name, I will do it" (John 14:14). It's my prayer that we will no longer settle for silence. God wants to answer our prayers more than we want them answered.

The reality is that there are people who love Jesus (and there is no doubt that Jesus loves them) but He doesn't like talking to them. I know that may sound harsh, but it's true. There are people in our lives that we love, yet we don't like talking to them because they don't have the right spirit. This woman in the gospel of Matthew came to Jesus with the wrong attitude, but fortunately, she didn't give up. She changed her approach, and verse 25 says that she "came again," left her drama at the door, and "worshipped Him."

GOD IS FROM MISSOURI

This next key is crucial. To be effective in prayer, we must be prepared to worship God *first*. Perhaps the importance of worship can be better explained by the Missouri state motto. In fact, through my exegetical, hermeneutical, theological, and philosophical studies, I have come to believe (jokingly, of course!) that God is actually from Missouri! Why? Because,

Missouri is the "Show Me" State!

People can say, "I love you, Lord" all day long, but God's response is always, "Show Me!" Our love for God isn't unique. Golden retrievers love the Lord! Jersey cows love the Lord! What separates us from the rest of creation that truly "loves the Lord" is our unique capacity to worship. Even the angels in all their might and beauty cannot worship like those who have been redeemed by the blood of the Lamb. We can show God our love for Him through our worship. The worship of the redeemed, swelling up from a heart set toward God, has no equal.

Many Christians mentally agree with the idea of worship, but very few actually prepare for worship. Worship is often considered something reserved for the "super-spiritual," but it is much more practical than we might expect.

Preparation is the difference between success and failure in prayer; it is also the difference between success and failure in worship. How do we prepare for worship? Most don't "prepare" for worship at all! It's no wonder they don't know what to say! There are some steps we can take that will help us show God our love for Him.

Make a list. First, take some time to think about all of God's attributes that truly mean something to you. Who is God to you? Write it down! Jesus asked His disciples this same question:

> *When Jesus came into the coasts of Caesarea Philippi, he asked his disciples, saying, Whom do men say that I the Son of man am? And they said, Some say that thou art John the Baptist: some, Elias; and others, Jeremias, or one of the prophets. He saith unto them, But whom say ye that I am? And Simon Peter*

121

answered and said, Thou art the Christ, the Son of the living God (Matthew 16:13–16, emphasis added).

Here are some examples of the types of attributes you might put on that list:

The Great Physician	The Good Shepherd
My Comforter	The Prince of Peace
My Strong Tower	My High Priest
Faithful	My Substitute

Peter answered Jesus, "Thou art the Christ." This revelation didn't come from what someone had told him about God. Peter professed what had been revealed to him by his heavenly Father. Make your list personal. Have you experienced Him as Healer? Has He given you peace in the middle of a great trial? Who has He been to you in your life? To begin with, list between five and ten divine attributes and how they have affected your life—from His grace and mercy to His power and authority. This list will grow over time and so will your ability to worship.

Once you have your list, be sure to write down *why* these divine attributes matter to you. What is your testimony? Why are you thankful that He is your Healer? Is it because the doctors diagnosed you with cancer, but you went to the Great Physician and now you are cancer free? Are you thankful because you've never had cancer? Why are you thankful for His grace? For each attribute, write two or three short sentences about why you are thankful for it. Now we're getting somewhere!

Find supporting Bible verses. The next step is to find Bible verses that extol these particular characteristics. The book of Psalms is overflowing with this kind of worship. Write these verses down. Be sure to take your time with these first steps. Time spent in preparation is never wasted. Once you have written these things down, you are prepared to worship! If you're worried about this taking away from the normal, exuberant and unpredictable worship you're used to experiencing don't be. This kind of preparation and organization will actually add to the organic nature of your worship.

> **TIME SPENT IN PREPARATION IS NEVER WASTED.**

Use the list and the verses to worship God. Now you are prepared to worship. Begin by thanking God for the aspects of His divine nature that you've written down, continue by reading the corresponding verses aloud, and finish by telling Him what they've meant to you personally.

People inevitably ask, "How long should I worship?" The answer is simple: You should worship until you have the assurance that He has inhabited your praise (Psalm 22:3), and that He has approved of your worship with His presence. This assurance may come by being able to tangibly sense the presence of God or through an inward knowing and peace. Either way, there's no mistaking when the presence of God shows up.

This is what the Syrophoenician woman did when she realized that her "drama" wasn't getting God's attention. She needed a different approach if she hoped to receive anything at all from Jesus. Likewise, there is really no reason for us to pray at all, for any need, until we have God's attention. And the way to get His attention is through worship.

Read on, and I will tell you about a worship experience I had in my early days of ministry.

CHAPTER 11: QUESTIONS FOR REFLECTION

1. What percentage of your prayer effort is focused on asking God to fix problems or intervene in a crisis? What percentage of your time with God is spent developing and enjoying a relationship with Him? How would you like to see this change?

2. Do the people you currently associate with inspire you to seek more of God, or do they drain spiritual life from you? What can you do about this?

3. How does worship affect your prayer life? Why is it important to worship God?

4. Which of God's attributes are most meaningful to you? Why?

Chapter 12

PRAYER AND PRESENCE

"But if you make yourselves at home with me and my words are at home in you, you can be sure that whatever you ask will be listened to and acted upon" (John 15:7, MSG).

"Worship and intercession must go together; one is impossible without the other" —Oswald Chambers[1]

Two men were walking down a long dusty road, enjoying the evening and talking about everything under the sun. The subject of religion came up, and one challenged the other, "If you are so religious, let's hear you quote the Lord's Prayer. In fact, I bet you $10 that you can't."

The second responded, "Now I lay me down to sleep, I pray the Lord my

---

1 Oswald Chambers, "Oswald Chambers Quote: "Worship and Intercession Must Go Together, the One Is Impossible without the Other." *Quotefancy*, accessed February 06, 2019, https://quotefancy.com/quote/883071/Oswald-Chambers-Worship-and-intercession-must-go-together-the-one-is-impossible-without.

soul to keep. If I die before I wake, I pray the Lord my soul to take."

The first pulled out his wallet and fished out a ten-dollar bill, muttering, "I didn't think you could do it!"[2]

THE DIRTY DOZEN

I can remember a time early in my ministry life when I was given the task of taking over the organization and planning of my church's monthly prayer meeting. At the time, we met once a month on Saturday nights to pray for our ministry.

PRAYER IS "WORK" AND IT REQUIRES A MATURE CHRISTIAN TO RECOGNIZE ITS WORTH IN COMPARISON TO COMPETING PRIORITIES.

Prayer meetings aren't always the most highly attended church events. The reasons for this are twofold. First, we know that Satan hates prayer, and he will do what he can to distract believers from what causes his kingdom the most damage. Secondly, we know that prayer is "work" and it requires a mature Christian to recognize its worth in comparison to competing priorities. To see the real size of a church, don't look at who's showing up on Sunday morning, look at who's showing up for Tuesday night prayer meetings. This will reveal the true backbone of that ministry.

2 Dave Martin, "How to Pray," *Sermon Central*, April 23, 2002, accessed February 06, 2019, https://www.sermoncentral.com/sermons/how-to-pray-dave-martin-sermon-on-prayer-how-to-45836?ref=SermonSerps.

When I was given the opportunity to begin leading these prayer meetings, we had about a dozen people attending. Needless to say, it wasn't a very promising gig for an aspiring young minister who dreamed of preaching to the masses! Nevertheless, it was in preparation for one of these little prayer meetings that God began to teach me the importance of worship.

Until this time, all twelve of us would show up, pray fervently over a specific list of prayer requests, and then go home having accomplished our good deed for the day. I remember it very clearly. On the Monday following my first official prayer meeting as the leader, I began to sense that we needed to try a different approach in the next prayer meeting. I had this overwhelming sense that all He wanted us to do was to worship Him. I quickly called some eager Bible college students who were studying worship, and asked them if they would be willing to help out by providing a time of worship. They were ecstatic.

As the days passed, there was a growing anticipation in my spirit. I felt like something magnificent was going to happen. That month seemed to move more slowly than molasses on a winter day. I knew that God had something special in store for us, but I didn't quite know what it was.

The night before the prayer meeting, I couldn't sleep. I dreamed that all of a sudden hundreds would be drawn by the Holy Spirit to this prayer meeting like the animals were drawn to the ark! I couldn't wait to see what God was going to do.

As the prayer meeting started, I was even more confused. All I saw were the same dirty dozen we had last month! There we were: a rag-tag worship team that didn't know what they were doing, and their fearless leader (me) who was just as clueless, looking out at the masses who weren't there.

Sometimes, when God begins to reveal His plan to us, we get our wires crossed and think He intends to do it all overnight. What He really wants to do is build a sturdy foundation in our lives so that what He has planned doesn't become a flash in the pan. I've learned over the years that God is never in a hurry.

All I had was one instruction from the Holy Spirit: Worship! So we did. We worshiped for what felt like forever, and the people were getting restless. I was sure they were thinking, "We came to pray, and I wish we'd get to it! I have a roast waiting in the crockpot at home!" Finally, I decided that we needed to take a break from the worship for a moment. I whispered a little prayer to God, "Okay, Lord, I'm going to have a riot on my hands if we don't pray for *something*. We will do one more song, and then..." But before I could finish the sentence, something happened!

I felt a release in the people's worship. It seemed like they began to forget about their own prayer needs and began to worship from their hearts. It was as though everyone got their second wind at the same time. We had unknowingly managed to push through the cares and worries of our own personal lives, and place our entire focus on God.

Nothing else mattered, and when we got to that place, God was there waiting on us! His presence was evident to all who came that night; and as we began to pray, we noticed an effortlessness that had not previously been there. When God gets involved, He takes the work out of prayer. It only seemed like a few moments, but when we looked up it was already after midnight!

We were changed. We didn't care how many might come the next month. We just couldn't wait to get together again to worship God and be in His presence. Strangely enough, at the next meeting, we had double the attendance. Then the next month, we had double again. At times, we had hundreds who gathered with us to seek God in passionate worship!

Learning to wait on God in prayer through worship will take the struggle out of our daily prayer life. If we learn to worship first, we'll discover that in the presence of God, difficult things become easy. We will discover that all that drama we were once worried about will become insignificant.

THE WORD OF GOD

In order to understand prayer—the true nature of prayer—it would help if we would just forget everything we think we know about the subject. In the words of Yoda, "You must unlearn what you have learned!"[3] Much of what we call prayer in today's Americanized, bumper sticker, Christian philosophy of prayer can be broken up into several distinct categories:

The Negotiator's Prayer: The Negotiator attempts to bribe God by offering Him a great deal: "God, if you'll just get me out of this, I promise to go to church this Sunday!"

The Blackmailer's Prayer: The Blackmailer isn't as polite as the Negotiator. He's done playing nice with God, and now he's determined to make God an offer He can't refuse: "God, if you don't answer this prayer, I'll

---

3 "Yoda Quotes," *Yoda Quotes* – Largest Collection Of Master Yoda Quotes On The Internet, accessed February 06, 2019, http://www.yodaquotes.net/you-must-unlearn-what-you-have-learned.

never go to church again!"

The Pious Prayer: The Pious Prayer is generally offered exclusively for the sake of an audience. Whether it's with a church group, over Thanksgiving dinner, or solely for conscience's sake, the purpose of this prayer is to make others think we are spiritual or holy. You can tell if you're guilty of praying this type of prayer if you're unable to recall the prayer you prayed two minutes after you say amen.

The Pity Prayer: The Pity Prayer is probably the most popular of all the nonstarters. "Lord, I'm so desperate; if You don't do something, I'm not going to make it!" This prayer feels the need to show God pictures of malnourished children, the crumbling foundations of our homes, or the buckets of tears we've shed. After all, if we can "sell" God on how desperate our need is, He will have to respond, right?

Wrong, wrong, wrong. God's not looking to make a deal, associate with religious icons, or listen to a sales pitch. God is looking for worshipers. God is looking for people who will make His presence their priority, and who will consider time with Him more precious than silver or gold.

When we take the time to worship Him first, we will sense the presence of God right there where we are. At times, God's presence will come to us like a rushing wind or a mighty fire, and at other times, it will come as a still small voice or an inner witness. Either way, we will know that God is near.

Once we have the assurance and peace that comes from knowing that God is near, it's time to speak the Word. We must be careful not to begin to speak our own words. The Holy Spirit is like a dove, and He is very particular about where He rests. Our Creator is looking for someone to agree with:

"Can two walk together, except they be agreed?" (Amos 3:3).

Remember when Jesus was walking with His disciples along the coast of Caesarea Philippi (Matthew 16:15) and He asked them, "Who do you say that I am?" What was the purpose of this question? Did Jesus have amnesia? Did He forget who He was? Of course not! He was looking for someone to agree with Him, because agreement is the way He gains access into our lives.

HE WAS LOOKING FOR SOMEONE TO AGREE WITH HIM, BECAUSE AGREEMENT IS THE WAY HE GAINS ACCESS INTO OUR LIVES.

According to Genesis 1 and Psalm 8, God placed us in authority in the earth. Therefore, if God desires to do anything significant in the earth, He must get us to agree with Him. This is the purpose of prayer! Our heavenly Father needs to find someone to say, "Thy will be done in earth, as it is in heaven" (Matthew 6:10).

Agreement with God is the essence of true prayer. All prayer must begin with the Word of God; and the desired end of each prayer must be the fulfillment of the will of God. Unless we grasp this simple, yet revolutionary principle, we will not find much success in prayer. Prayer is all about agreeing with God and His Word.

We must learn to speak God's Word and not our own. As we prepare for prayer, the Bible verses we need don't always suddenly come to us out of the blue. We can prepare for success in prayer by writing down the verses that articulate the will of God for our lives. Once the presence of God shows up, we can begin to speak those verses aloud and praise God for His Word.

LEARNING HIS WAYS

Getting into the presence of God is easy. God desires to be with us so much more than we desire to be with Him. He has made all the preparations and stands ready to greet us. Abiding in the presence of God can be effortless—if we first learn His ways.

> *"I don't think the way you think.*
> *The way you work isn't the way I work."*
> *God's Decree.*
> *"For as the sky soars high above earth,*
> *so the way I work surpasses the way you work,*
> *and the way I think is beyond the way you think.*
> *Just as rain and snow descend from the skies*
> *and don't go back until they've watered the earth,*
> *Doing their work of making things grow and blossom,*
> *producing seed for farmers and food for the hungry,*
> *So will the words that come out of my mouth*
> *not come back empty-handed.*
> *They'll do the work I sent them to do,*
> *they'll complete the assignment I gave them"*
> *(Isaiah 55:10–11, MSG).*

Learning His ways, seeking His face, and experiencing His glory is what it's all about. However, many never get over the first hurdle of learning His ways, and they become like "broken cisterns, that can hold no water" (Jeremiah 2:13).

Without an understanding of the ways of God, we are nothing more than fractured vessels that cannot contain the glory of God.

It's said that if you give a man a fish you can feed him for a day, but if you teach a man to fish, you can feed him for a lifetime. Instead of looking for a quick fix, we must learn to sustain spiritual things. Accidental victory is no guarantee of future success.

In times of distress, loss, or grief, we will invariably hear pious parrots squawking on about how His ways are not our ways, and His thoughts are not our thoughts. To these folks, divine transcendence is something to be admired, but this gap between humanity and deity is nothing to be praised. The breach between God's ways and ours is a problem, not a providence. This fissure is the reason for creation's chaos; yet many quote it as though it should provide some sort of comfort for the confused. We hear things like, "In this time of loss, it's difficult to understand, but His ways are not our ways."

This direct dereliction of doctrine would almost be tolerable if it weren't so preposterous. In this verse, God, through Isaiah, clearly explains that there is a cure for this malady of separation: the Word! It is true that God's thoughts are heavenly while ours are often grounded, but, just as rain and snow descend from the skies and don't go back until they've watered the earth, so God will send His Word. Gideon's cry is always based on God's Word.

What is a word? A word is a thought communicated. God, in His grace, bridges the gap between His thoughts and our thoughts with His Word. Now we can make His ways our ways through the revelation of the Word of God.

Isn't that what the gospel is all about? God sent His Son—the Word made flesh—to bridge the gap. How do we stay on track when we're seeking God in prayer? The Word! How do we align our thoughts with His? The Word. The Word must saturate our prayer life. When the Word is not only the basis of our prayers, but the answer to them as well, we're on our way to victory.

CHAPTER 12: QUESTIONS FOR REFLECTION

1. Have there been times when you felt the supernatural presence of God? Describe what it was like.

2. Have you ever spent time worshiping before you began praying about your needs? What kind of difference does this make?

3. Have you ever found yourself praying in any of the four ways described in this chapter? How is prayer defined in this chapter?

4. According to Isaiah 55:11, how can we bridge the gap between God's thoughts and our thoughts?

Chapter 13

THE PRIMACY OF PURPOSE

"The coming revival must begin with a great revival of prayer. It is in the closet, with the door shut, that the sound of abundance of rain will first be heard. An increase of secret prayer with ministers will be the sure harbinger of blessing." —Andrew Murray[1]

"Brace yourself for a shock. Something's about to take place and you're going to find it hard to believe" (Habakkuk 1:5, MSG).

It was the 1860s. Ministers from all over Cape Town, South Africa, gathered to pray for a revival. Since their hearts were in the right place, and God is more eager to send a revival than we are to receive it, they didn't have to wait long. One Sunday in a youth service, everyone was invited to pray as

---

1 Andrew Murray, "Entire Quotes Database," *ChristianQuotes.info*, accessed February 06, 2019, https://www.christianquotes.info/search-for-a-quote/#axzz5ehy3hSwB.

they were led by the Spirit. A young fifteen-year-old African girl responded and cried out in faith-filled passion for God to visit His church once again.

One eyewitness said, "While she was praying, we heard a sound in the distance, which came nearer and nearer, until the whole hall seemed to shake. The entire congregation began to call on God, and the noise was deafening." As a fearful awareness of God filled the hearts of those in prayer that day, they became oblivious to their surroundings, and each one began to cry out themselves.

As things began to intensify, the senior pastor, who was attending to other duties at the time but had been praying for revival, walked in. He, not immediately recognizing this as the answer to his heart's cry, was appalled at the chaotic scene and demanded that it stop immediately. No one listened. The pastor insisted, "People, be silent! God is a God of order, and this is confusion!" Everyone was so captivated by the presence of God that no one paid him any attention.

The pastor stormed out of the prayer meeting, confused and concerned for his congregation. Before long there were three prayer meetings like this a day. They would always start out normal enough, but then there would be a sound of a rushing wind that would fill the place. Some fell prostrate under the anointing of the Holy Spirit while others cried out in repentance.

During one meeting, the pastor was about to attempt to shut it down once again when a respected friend visiting from America said to him, "Be careful what you do! I have come from America, where revival has been moving.

This is precisely what I have witnessed there. This is the Spirit of God."[2]

The pastor's heart was transformed in that moment as he opened his church and his heart to the radical moving of the Spirit of God in prayer. That pastor's name was Andrew Murray.

From major cities to remote plantations and villages, the power of God was released through passionate prayer. We now know Andrew Murray as an apostle of prayer, having written such Christian classics as *With Christ in the School of Prayer*[3], but it wasn't always that way. At one point, with all his biblical education, Murray himself was resistant to the very revival for which he was praying.

Much later, Andrew Murray's ministerial friends would lovingly goad him saying, "Hey, Brother Andrew, tell us about that revival you tried to stop." Looking back on those days in his book entitled *Humility*, Murray wrote: "If only we did not so often hinder Him with our much trying to serve, how surely and mightily would He accomplish His own work of renewing souls into the likeness of Jesus Christ."[4]

In his younger years, Andrew Murray thought if the Holy Spirit were going to move, it would have to be through him. This is the folly of many ministries and the failure of many revivals. We must cling to the tried and tested principles of prayer that we know, but we must also understand that

---

2 J. Du Plessis, "The Life of Andrew Murray of South Africa," – Dated 1919; Brought by the School of Prayer's Founder, Peter-John Parisis of Linden, Michigan (Bryan Edwin Dean; Harry Walter Dean and Margaret Lenore Dean's Son): J. Du Plessis & Andrew Murray: Free Download, Borrow, and Streaming," Full Text of "Passing", accessed February 06, 2019, https://archive.org/details/TheLifeOfAndrewMurrayOfSouthAfrica-ByJ.DuPlessis-Dated1919.

3 Andrew Murray, *With Christ in the School of Prayer* (Springdale, PA: Whitaker House, December 1, 1981).

4 *Revival Fires: Stirring Accounts of Christian Revivals around the World* (Northampton: Jesus Fellowship Resources, 1996).

the answer to our prayers may not always look the way we think it should.

Just before his departure from this world, Smith Wigglesworth prophesied to a young evangelist named Lester Sumrall about the last days. He said this: "I see the greatest revival in the history of mankind coming to Planet Earth, maybe as never before. And I see every form of disease healed. I see whole hospitals emptied with no one there. Even the doctors are running down the streets shouting.

He told me that there would be untold numbers of uncountable multitudes that would be saved. No man will say 'so many, so many' because nobody will be able to count those who come to Jesus. No disease will be able to stand before God's people... It will be a worldwide situation, not local," he said, "a worldwide thrust of God's power and God's anointing upon mankind." Then he opened his eyes and looked at me and said, "I will not see it, but you shall see it."[5]

Concerning revival, Dr. Lester Sumrall often said:

"Most people are not capable of going from blessing to blessing. Most denominations and people die in the same revelation they first received from God. Many of the people who call themselves Lutherans are living in the same blessing Luther had 400 years ago. Often, the people calling themselves Wesleyan or Methodist are living in the blessing of Wesley a couple of hundred years ago. It is difficult to get themselves out of a groove or a system."[6]

---

5 Andrew Strom, "GREAT HEALING REVIVALISTS - HOW GOD'S POWER CAME.," accessed February 06, 2019, http://www.evanwiggs.com/revival/portrait/healing.html, quoted from Lester Sumrall, *Pioneers of Faith* (Tulsa, OK: Harrison House, 1995), 168-169.
6 Lester Sumrall, "I Saw the Glory, My Relationship with Smith Wigglesworth" (speech, Sermon).

We must be guided by the past, not blinded by it. One of the easiest things for a student of revival to do is to worship the past, instead of learning from it. This is nothing new. When Hezekiah began to reign in Judah, he saw the need for moral awakening (2 Kings 18). The people had grossly defiled themselves, incurring the wrath of God. What did Hezekiah do? He attacked his enemy head-on. Who was this foe?

Hezekiah had an unusual adversary in his campaign to restore God's blessing to the nation. It was a brass serpent named Nehushtan. This was no pagan idol made by some barbarian.

ONE OF THE EASIEST THINGS FOR A STUDENT OF REVIVAL TO DO IS TO WORSHIP THE PAST, INSTEAD OF LEARNING FROM IT.

This was the very same brass serpent that had been made by Moses in the wilderness (Numbers 21:4–9). At that time, the Jewish people had tested God's patience one time too many, and their lack of gratitude became unbearable, so God allowed an army of serpents to invade the camp. As Moses stood in brave intercession for the people, God's mercy prevailed, and a remedy was provided: Moses was to construct a pole with a bronze serpent wrapped around it. Everyone who looked upon it, though they had been bitten by the serpents and had venom coursing through their veins, lived. The commanding image of the serpent on the pole became, in this historic moment, a reminder and a representation of God's power. This brazen serpent became known as Nehushtan.

God's chosen people learned from their mistakes, were healed, and entered into the Promised Land. What happened to Nehushtan? It was merely an instrument used by God as a point of contact for a moment to release His power. After the moment had passed, in God's eyes the item was obsolete. But, as often happens, we tend to turn the obsolete into idols. Years later, in direct violation of the second commandment, the serpent became an object of worship.

Today we must learn from our past and walk confidently in the trail blazed by our forefathers, but we must be cautious not to allow these memorials to become idols. The individuals and events of the past should represent starting blocks for us, not a finish line. God is not limited to using the Nehushtans of the past. Gideon's cry seeks the same power, through the same divine Word, *but through any means God chooses.* For many, their brazen serpent is their church or their denomination, but God may use the most unlikely of avenues for His blessing. We must be willing to jump in wherever He is working.

To receive a spiritual awakening for his nation, Hezekiah had to destroy the idol of their past. Many today are pickled by nostalgia, and our memories have become formaldehyde. We can't be content to live in an afterglow if we wish to cry out for fresh fire. The best way to honor the memory of these great revivals and revivalists is to follow their example and walk in the courage to do something no one in their generation had ever seen before. We need to ask God right now to identify any idols we may have in our lives.

When Elijah made his fiery exit and Elisha took up the mantle, Elijah's enthusiasts were standing on the other side of the river waiting for their hero to return (2 Kings 2:11–18). Elisha raised his master's mantle over his head, smote the waters, and the Jordan River parted. The river made no distinction between Elijah and Elisha. The Elijah groupies, however, were another matter; they wanted Elijah the man, not the anointing of his mantle.

They begged Elisha to let them go look for Elijah's body because they suspected that the Spirit had dropped him on a mountain somewhere. The church has to stop looking for Elijah's body and likewise stop mourning over Saul (1 Samuel 16:1)! If we don't become wise to this fact, altars of fire will become artifacts, ministries will become museums, miracles will become methods, and God's people will end up powerless.

We're not supposed to be seeking Elijah. We're supposed to be seeking the *God* of Elijah (2 Kings 2:14). Gideon's cry is looking for a mantle, not a man. We don't need another John Wesley. What we need is another encounter with John Wesley's God. We don't need another Dwight L. Moody. We don't need another Wigglesworth, another Finney, or another Andrew Murray. What we do need is an encounter with the God of these revivalists—and a revival that transforms us and everyone around us.

I don't know what this encounter will look like, but I do know that the casual and the predictable cannot contain or sustain it. It may not be loud and dramatic like George Whitefield, or written and legible like Johnathan Edwards, but I can almost guarantee that it will be the opposite of what makes us comfortable.

God is about to speak to us about our next level of power and presence. Are we listening? We often have difficulty hearing from God because He always talks about conquest and victory, while we tend to think about survival and preservation. God speaks to us about confrontation, while we often avoid it at all costs. God speaks to us about a plan that will carry us into the unknown, while we want all the details laid out for us ahead of time. Are we really listening, or are we just listening for what we want to hear? I'm sure that the apostle Paul wanted God's plan to make him popular, but instead it often landed him in prison.

Gideons must ask themselves if they really want God's answer to the question they've been asking: "Where is the power?" Do we really want to know, or do we have a natural aversion to hearing what God really wants to say to us? Oh, what a freeing thing it is to finally allow God to be honest with us!

What do we do when God's answer doesn't look like what we thought it would? The prophet Elijah told the king and his servant that a mighty out-pouring of rain was coming, but when the servant went to look for it, all he saw was a "a little cloud out of the sea, like a man's hand" (1 Kings 18:44). In Joel 2, God promised a mighty outpouring of His Spirit:

And it shall come to pass afterward, that I will pour out my spirit upon all flesh; and your sons and your daughters shall prophesy, your old men shall dream dreams, your young men shall see visions: and also upon the servants and upon the handmaids in those days will I pour out my spirit. And I will shew wonders in the heavens and in the earth, blood, and fire, and pillars of smoke. The sun shall be turned into darkness, and the moon into blood, before the great and terrible day of the LORD come. And it shall come to pass, that whosoever shall call on the name of the LORD shall be delivered: for in mount Zion and in Jerusalem shall be deliverance, as the Lord hath said, and in the remnant whom the Lord shall call (Joel 2:28–32).

In Acts 2, we see the fulfillment of this prophecy, but it didn't look like we might have expected it to look:

And when the day of Pentecost was fully come, they were all with one accord in one place. And suddenly there came a sound from heaven as of a rushing mighty wind, and it filled all the house where they were sitting. And there appeared unto them cloven tongues like as of fire, and it sat upon each of them. And they were all filled with the Holy Ghost, and began to speak with other tongues, as the Spirit gave them utterance (Acts 2:1–4).

No wonder some—who were learned in the Scriptures—mocked Peter's message that day (Acts 2:13). Are we willing to accept God's answer, even if it shows up riding a donkey instead of a stallion?

Tommy Hicks was a powerful healing evangelist who brought a revival to Argentina in the 1950s that saw hundreds of thousands of conversions and miraculous healings. After that revival, Tommy Hicks had a vision of a great awakening in the last days. I believe this to be very instructive, so I've included the full vision in the appendix of this book. Tommy Hicks saw a mighty church rising out of the ashes performing the works of Jesus Christ. He saw Jesus stretch forth His hand towards His followers, offering them the power to heal, deliver, and save. Here is a portion of that vision:

"And I beheld this Christ as He continued to stretch forth His Hand; but there was a tragedy. There were many people, as He stretched forth His

Hand, who refused the anointing of God and the call of God.

I saw men and women whom I knew. People whom I felt would certainly receive the call of God. But as He stretched forth His Hand toward this one and toward that one, they simply bowed their heads and began to back away. And each of those who seemed to bow down and back away, seemed to go into darkness. Blackness seemed to swallow them everywhere. I was bewildered as I watched it, but these people that he had anointed, hundreds of thousands of people all over the world, in Africa, England, Russia, China, America, all over the world, the anointing of God was upon these people as they went forward in the name of the Lord.[7]

Dear Christian, don't back away from what God has called us to do. It may seem daunting and uncomfortable, but that's why He sent the Comforter to help us. We've identified the barriers to power in the Christian's life. We've even talked about practical things we can do to avail ourselves of God's power in prayer, but there is no substitute for a heart after God. David declared, "As the hart panteth after the water brooks, so panteth my soul after thee, O God" (Psalm 42:1).

Gideon may not have had the best education, he may have allowed sin in his life, and he probably didn't know all these prayer principles, but he did have a passion for the power of God. A heart that burns for God can accomplish more than all the training in the world. It can unlock the mercy of God that enables us to overcome every other obstacle we face.

Do we want it? Are we willing to see the pursuit of it as our purpose in

---

7 Tommy Hicks, "Revivalist Tommy Hicks' End-Times Vision of the Army of God," *Destiny Encounters International*, March 31, 2018, , accessed February 06, 2019, https://www.destinyencounters.com/news/2018/3/31/revivalist-tommy-hicks-end-times-vision-of-the-army-of-god.

life? Billy Sunday said, "More men fail through lack of purpose than lack of talent."[8] I would add *passion* to that as well. What are we willing to give for it? Are we willing to make the pursuit of it our singular purpose and allow everything else to orbit around its gravitational pull? If we are, it's time to be recommissioned.

Not long ago, my son and I went on a unique trip in which we were able to spend the night on a giant aircraft carrier, the U.S.S. Yorktown. This massive ship had been built during World War II and seen some major action throughout the years leading up to, and including, the Vietnam War. The U.S.S. Yorktown had earned eleven battle stars and the Presidential Unit Citation for its work in the Pacific Theater. We were in awe as they walked us through her heroic history. This ship had been built for battle!

Though she was decommissioned after World War II, when the need arose, she was modernized and recommissioned in the 1950s as an attack carrier. She even assisted in the recovery of the Apollo 8 space mission. After an illustrious carrier, the U.S.S. Yorktown became a movie prop in the classic war movie, *Tora! Tora! Tora!* and the science fiction film, *The Philadelphia Experiment.* Later, she was decommissioned once again and became a museum at Patriot's Point, Mount Pleasant, South Carolina. Today, she is a National Historic Landmark.

Honestly, it was a little sad to see a ship, originally created for combat, now full of snotty-nosed kids using her weapons as a jungle gym. The U.S.S. Yorktown was created for a singular purpose, but it has now been officially decommissioned and is a recreational spot for tourists. You, too, have been

8 Billy Sunday, "Billy Sunday Quotes," BrainyQuote, accessed February 06, 2019, https://www.brainyquote.com/quotes/billy_sunday_129120.

created by God for a particular purpose that centers around conflict. Sadly, it seems that the modern church has been officially decommissioned. Now, instead of training believers for the battle, we're focused on catering to tourists and spiritual children who refuse to grow up. It's time to embrace our purpose and look to the future. No more dwelling on the past. Gideon's cry doesn't dwell on questions like, "What could have been?"

A man named Lot, who lived in Sodom, had plenty of reasons for regret. His mind was so warped by his past failures and his present circumstances that he had to be convinced by angels to leave the doomed city in which he lived. When he left, he was given one instruction: "Don't look back!"

It's easy to become so consumed with our past that we miss what God is doing right now. Esau was condemned for trading his future for instant gratification (Hebrews 12:16). David had to be reminded by Abigail to focus on his future (1 Samuel 25:28–33). Jesus Himself wept over the city of Jerusalem, because they knew not the hour of their visitation (Luke 19:41–44).

Timing and focus are everything. The Bible says, "Seek ye the LORD while he may be found" and "call ye upon him while he is near" (Isaiah 55:6). So often, we frolic in trivial pursuits as the stage is being set before us for the greatest evangelistic opportunity in history.

This is our time. Maybe we've prayed before, but it's time to pray again. The windows of heaven are open right now. All we have to do is rise up, reach out, and receive.

The story of Gideon speaks volumes to us. Gideon was not cowardly, and neither are we. Gideon was frustrated because of the inconsistencies of his time compared to the eternal truth of God's Word. This frustration, pain, and anger often becomes the epicenter of radical change in our lives. God certainly doesn't send these things to change us; but sadly, the only time many of us will ever take time to depend on Him is in dire situations.

This is an important distinction. In church circles, we like to talk and sing about how "trials come to make us strong," but that's simply not true. The reality is that trials come to kill, steal, and destroy, but repentance and reliance on the Word of God makes us strong.

TRIALS COME TO KILL, STEAL, AND DESTROY, BUT REPENTANCE AND RELIANCE ON THE WORD OF GOD MAKES US STRONG.

Think about it: If trials really made us strong, then we'd all be superheroes! We may think that some difficult event we went through made us a wiser or better person, but if we really look back on it, that event was crushing us until we turned to God and His Word. It was only then that we became wiser and stronger.

Trouble comes knocking on all our doors. We can't control everything that happens in our lives, but we can control our reaction to it. In the time of our greatest need, we can choose to stand on the Word and rise above the circumstances, or we can allow them to control us and crush us.

Gideon threshing wheat was like Moses killing the Egyptian. He was taking care of an immediate need but disregarding a greater purpose. Without understanding our purpose, we'll always try to accomplish with the arm of the flesh what God has called us to do by His Spirit.

God redirected Gideon and supernaturally reminded him of what He had called him to accomplish. My prayer for you is that you won't have to wait to hear from an angelic messenger before you begin to do all God has planned for you. May your encounter with God be no less life-changing than Gideon's. May Gideon's cry be your cry—and may God graciously grant you the answers you seek, according to His Word.

CHAPTER 13: QUESTIONS FOR REFLECTION

1. Has there ever been a time when you were reluctant to believe that something was from God simply because you had never seen it before? Discuss this.

2. Describe a time when God was honest with you—about you. What did He say? Did it make you uncomfortable? What did you do about it?

3. Talk about a time you experienced trouble, and how you reacted to it. What would you change if that situation occurred again?

4. Gideon's cry was to see the power of God at work in his generation. What is the cry of your heart today?

APPENDIX - TOMMY HICKS' VISION

Tommy Hicks was an American healing revivalist who rose to fame in the Argentinian revivals of 1954. He secured a meeting with President Juan Perón to ask permission to hold a salvation and healing crusade in the country. After requesting and receiving prayer, Perón himself was healed of a long-standing skin condition. This prompted him to give Tommy Hicks access to the largest stadium in the country, where overflowing crowds came and received ministry. Over a two-month period, three million people had attended his meetings, with 300,000 decisions for Christ and many, many healings reported.

This attracted the attention of the Full Gospel Business Men's Fellowship, which became a large financial backer for his revival meetings.

In 1961, he received a "prophetic vision" of the end-times, which has been recounted many times. By permission, that vision is recorded here, to inspire your faith and encourage you in your walk with God.

"When this vision appeared to me, I suddenly found myself at a great height. I was looking down upon the earth, when suddenly the whole world came into view—every nation, every kindred, every tongue came before my sight. From the east and the west; from the north and the south; I recognized the countries and cities that I had been in. I was almost in fear and trembling as I stood beholding the great sight before me. At that moment, when the world came into view, it began to lightning and thunder.

"As the lightning flashed over the face of the earth, my eyes went downward and I was facing the north. Suddenly I beheld what looked like a great giant. As I stared and looked at it, I was almost bewildered by the sight. The giant was gigantic. His feet seemed to reach to the North Pole and his head to the South Pole. His arms were stretched from sea to sea. I could not even begin to understand whether this was a mountain or whether this was a giant. As I watched, I suddenly beheld that it was a great giant. I could see he was struggling for life, to even live. His body was covered with debris from head to foot; and at times this great giant would move his body and act as though he would rise up. When he did, thousands of little creatures seemed to run away. Hideous-looking creatures would run away from this giant and when he would become calm, they would come back.

"All of a sudden this great giant lifted one hand toward the heavens, and then he lifted his other hand. When he did, these creatures by the thousands seemed to flee away from this giant and go out into the night. Slowly this great giant began to rise, and as he did his head and hands went into the clouds. As he arose to his feet he seemed to have cleansed himself from the debris and filth that was upon him and he began to raise his hands into the heavens as though praising the Lord. As he raised his hands, they went even unto the clouds.

"Suddenly, every cloud became silver, the most beautiful silver that I have ever known. As I watched the phenomenon, it was so great, I could not even begin to understand what it all meant, I was so stirred as I watched it. I cried unto the Lord and I said, "Oh, Lord, what is the meaning of this?" And it felt as if I was actually in the Spirit and I could feel the presence of the Lord, even as I was asleep. From those clouds, suddenly there came great drops of liquid light raining down upon this mighty giant. Slowly, slowly, this giant began to melt—began to sink, as it were, into the very earth itself.

As he melted, his whole form seemed to have melted upon the face of the earth. This great rain began to come down. Liquid drops of light began to flood the very earth itself. As I watched this giant that seemed to melt, suddenly it became millions of people over the face of the earth. As I beheld the giant before me, people stood up all over the world. They were lifting their hands and they were praising the Lord.

"At that very moment there came a great thunder that seemed to roar from the heavens. I turned my eyes toward the heavens, and suddenly I saw a figure in white, in glistening white, but somehow I knew that it was the Lord Jesus Christ. He stretched forth His hand. As He did, He would stretch it forth to one, and to another, and to another; He stretched forth His hand upon the peoples and the nations of the world—men and women. As He pointed toward them, this liquid light seemed to flow from His hand into this person and a mighty anointing of God came upon them. Those people began to go forth in the name of the Lord. I do not know how long I watched it. It seemed it went into days and weeks and months. I beheld this Christ as He continued to stretch forth His hand. But there was a tragedy. There were many people, as He stretched forth His hands that refused the anointing of God and call of God. I saw men and women that I knew, people that I felt that certainly they would receive the call of God. As He stretched forth His hand toward this one, and towards that one, they simply bowed their heads and began to back away. To each of those that seemed to bow down and back away, they seemed to go into darkness. Blackness seemed to swallow them everywhere.

"I was bewildered as I watched it. These people that He had anointed covered the earth. There were hundreds of thousands of these people all over the world—in Africa, Asia, Russia, China, America, all over the world. The anointing of God was upon these people as they went forth in the name of the Lord. I saw these men and women as they went forth. They were ditch diggers; they were washer women; they were rich men; they were poor men. I saw people who were bound with paralysis and sickness, and blindness and deafness. As the Lord stretched forth His hand to give them this anointing, they became well, they became healed—and they went forth.

"This is the miracle of it. This is the glorious miracle of it. Those people would stretch forth their hands exactly as the Lord did, and it seemed that there was this same liquid fire that seemed to be in their hands. As they stretched forth their hands, they said, 'According to my word, be thou made whole.' As these people continued in this mighty end-time ministry, I did not fully realize what it was. I looked to the Lord and said, 'What is the meaning of this?' He said, 'This is that, that I will do in the last day. I will restore all the cankerworm, the palmerworm, the caterpillar—I will restore all that they have destroyed. This My people in the end-time, shall go forth; and as a mighty army, shall they sweep over the face of the earth.'

"As I was at this great height, I could behold the whole world. I watched these people as they were going to and fro over the face of the earth. Suddenly there was a man in Africa, and in a moment he was transported in the Spirit of God, and perhaps he was in Russia, or China, or America, or some other place, and vice versa. All over the world these people went. They came through fire and through pestilence and through famine. Neither fire nor persecution—nothing seemed to stop them. Angry mobs came to them with swords and with guns, and like Jesus, they passed through the multitude and they could not find them. But they went forth in the name of the

Lord. Everywhere they stretched forth their hands, the sick were healed, the blind eyes were opened. There was not a long prayer. I never saw a church, and I never saw or heard a denomination. These people were going in the name of the Lord of Hosts.

"As they marched forward as the ministry of Christ in the end-time, these people ministered to the multitudes over the face of the earth. Tens of thousands, even millions, seemed to come to the Lord Jesus Christ as these people stood forth and gave the message of the Kingdom—of the coming Kingdom in this last hour. It was so glorious! It seemed there were those that rebelled. They would become angry. They tried to attack those workers that were giving the message. God is going to give to the world a demonstration in this last hour such as the world has never known. These men and women are of all walks of life. Degrees will mean nothing. I saw these workers as they were going over the face of the earth. When one would seem to stumble and fall, another would come and pick him up. There were no big 'I' little 'you.' Every mountain was brought low and every valley was exalted, and they seemed to have one thing in common—there was a divine love that seemed to flow forth from these people as they went together, as they worked together, as they lived together. It was the theme of their lives. They continued and it seemed the days went by as I stood and beheld this sight. I could only cry—and sometimes I laughed.

"It was so wonderful as these people went throughout the face of the whole earth showing forth God's power in this last end-time. As I watched from the very heaven itself, there were times when great deluges of this liquid light seemed to fall upon great congregations. The congregations would lift their hands and seemingly praise God for hours and even days, as the

Spirit of God came upon them. God said, 'I will pour out My Spirit upon all flesh.' That is exactly the thing that God was doing. From every man and woman that received this power and the anointing of God, the miracles of God flowed continuously.

"Suddenly there was another great clap of thunder that seemed to resound around the world. Again I heard the voice saying: 'Now, this is My people; this is My beloved bride.' When the voice spoke, I looked upon the earth and I could see the lakes and the mountains. The graves were opened and people from all over the world, the saints of all ages, seemed to be rising. As they rose from the graves, suddenly all these people came from every direction, from the east and the west, from the north and the south, and they seemed to be forming again this gigantic body. As the dead in Christ seemed to be rising first, I could hardly comprehend it.

"It was so marvelous. It was so far beyond anything I could ever dream or think of. This huge body suddenly began to form and take shape again, and its shape was in the form of the mighty giant, but this time it was different. It was arrayed in the most beautiful, gorgeous white. Its garments were without spot or wrinkle as this body began to form, and the people of all ages seemed to be gathering into this body. Slowly, from the heavens above, the Lord Jesus came and became the head. I heard another clap of thunder that said, 'This is My beloved bride for whom I have waited. She will come forth, even tried by fire. This is she that I have loved from the beginning of time.' As I watched, my eyes turned to the far north and I saw great destruction, men and women in anguish and crying out, and buildings destroyed. Then I heard again, the fourth voice that said, 'Now My wrath being poured out upon the face of the earth.'

"From the ends of the whole world, it seemed that there were great vials of God's wrath being poured out upon the face of the earth. I can remember it as I beheld the awful sight of seeing cities, and whole nations going down into destruction. I could hear the weeping and the wailing. I could hear people crying. They seemed to cry as they went into caves, but the caves and the mountains opened up. They leaped in water, but the water would not drown them. There was nothing that seemingly could destroy them. They wanted to take their lives but they did not succeed.

"Again I turned my eyes toward the glorious sight of this body arrayed in the beautiful, white, shining garment. Slowly, slowly, it began to lift form the earth, and as it did, I awoke. This sight that I had beheld—I had seen the end-of-time ministry, the last hour. Again on July 27 at 2:30 in the morning the same revelation, the same vision, came again exactly as it did before. My life has been changed as I realize that we are living in that end time, for all over the world, God is anointing men and women with this ministry. It will not be doctrine. It will not be "churchianity"; but it is going to be Jesus Christ. They will give forth the word of the Lord and are going to say, I heard it so many times in the vision, 'According to my word, it shall be done.' Oh people, listen to me! 'According to my word, it shall be done.' We are going to be clothed with power and anointing from God. We won't have to preach sermons. We won't have to depend on man, nor will we be denominational echoes, but we will have the power of the living God! We will fear no man, but will go in the name of the Lord of Hosts!"[1]

---

1 Tommy Hicks, "Revivalist Tommy Hicks' End-Times Vision of the Army of God," Electronic Copyright © 2009 Tony Cauchi. www.revival-library.org. Reprinted by permission.

IF YOU'RE A FAN OF THIS BOOK, WILL YOU HELP ME SPREAD THE WORD?

There are several ways you can help me get the word out about the message of this book…

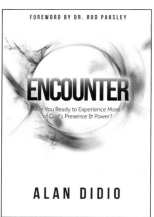

- Post a 5-star review on Amazon.

- Write about the book on your Facebook, Twitter, Instagram—any social media you regularly use!

- If you blog, consider referencing the book or publishing an excerpt from the book with a link back to my website. You have my permission to do this as long as you provide proper credit and backlinks.

- Recommend the book to friends—word-of-mouth is still the most effective form of advertising.

- Purchase additional copies to give away as gifts. You can do that by going to my website at: www.encountertoday.com

The best way to connect with me is to email through our website.

ENJOY THESE OTHER BOOKS BY ALAN DIDIO

Armed: Powerful Prayers for Perilous Times

It's time to storm the gates of hell with the power of the Spirit and the truth of the Scriptures. In these last days, God is calling the Church to respond with more than just hashtags and sympathies. God has given us an arsenal in the Spirit to help us live victoriously in perilous times. Lock and load. If you're going to be dangerous, you've got to first be ARMED.

Included in this Series:

- The Commanding Prayer

- The Avenging Prayer

- The Mystery of Prayer

- A Holy Invitation

- No More Hashtags

- How to Pray for the Peace of Jerusalem

**Purchase your copy from our store at
www.encountertoday.com**

ENJOY THESE OTHER MATERIALS BY ALAN DIDIO

Fish Come First (Digital Download with Bonus Materials)

In this renewed series (with BONUS materials) by Pastor Alan DiDio, you'll discover that the healing you desire, the deliverance you crave and the household salvation you long for is available in your wealthy place. Fish Come First is more than another teaching series, it is a Divine revelation that has changed many lives and will dramatically transform yours.

Included in this Series:

- A Draught of Fish (mp3)
- Fishers of Men (mp3)
- Miracles of Multiplication (mp3)
- 10 Keys to Entering Your Wealthy Place (mp3)
- Grace for Prosperity (mp4)

- Abounding Grace (mp4)
- Encounter Today Fish Come First Special (mp4)
- 101 Prosperity Confessions (pdf)
- 10 Debt Destroying Strategies (pdf)

Get access to your digital download right NOW when you visit our store at www.encountertoday.com

NEED A SPEAKER FOR YOUR NEXT PROGRAM?

Invite me to speak to your group or ministry. I have many years of public speaking experience. If you would like to have me come speak to your group, church or at an upcoming event, please contact me at: info@encountertoday.com

POSSIBLE SPEAKING TOPICS

- Revival

- Prayer

- Leadership

- Finances